Mount Up!

A MODERN DAY DELIVERANCE STORY

MOUNT UP!

How *One* Church Survived Hurricanes Katrina and Rita

PASTOR WILLIE L. MONNET, SR.

authorHOUSE®

AuthorHouse™
1663 Liberty Drive
Bloomington, IN 47403
www.authorhouse.com
Phone: 1-800-839-8640

First published by AuthorHouse 6/25/2010

ISBN: 978-1-4520-2416-5 (e)
ISBN: 978-1-4520-2415-8 (sc)
ISBN: 978-1-4520-2414-1 (hc)

Library of Congress Control Number: 2010907178

Printed in the United States of America
Bloomington, Indiana

This book is printed on acid-free paper.

"But they that wait upon the Lord shall renew their strength; they shall mount up with wings of eagles; they shall run, and not be weary; and they shall walk, and not faint."

Isaiah 40:31

CONTENTS

ACKNOWLEDGMENTS

First and foremost, we would like to give all praise, glory, honor, and thanks to our heavenly Father God, Jesus Christ our Savior, and our guide the Holy Spirit. We also would like to thank former President George W. Bush, Jr. for his assistance in the overall process. We would like to extend a special thanks to Pastor Richard Vaughn and his wife of Fletcher Emanuel Church Alive and the Conference and Retreat Center staff and volunteers for all of their hospitality, as well as coordinators Brian and Vickie Lane; Mrs. Bab; Mrs. Diane; Jacob and Luke; Hardin County Judge Billy Caraway; Mr. Will Moursen, Mr. McDonald, CEO of Texas Home Health; Lumberton Fire and Rescue Department; Lumberton ISD and students; Lumberton Lady Raiders Basketball Team; Robin Mauer, manager of Skate N Stuff, the manager and staff of Texas State Bank in Lumberton; the Red Onion Restaurant; the area churches of Hardin and Orange Countries, as well as Beaumont; and the generous people of Hardin County.

We also would like to extend special thanks to the staff at Lakeview Baptist Assembly Retreat Center (Lone Star), the Holiday Inn Select (Dallas Love Airport – especially the breakfast cooks), the administrative staff and sales department at AmeriSuites (Austin), Canyon of Eagle Retreat Center (Burnet), Woodward Hotel and Conference Center (Austin), Holiday Inn Express (Burnet), Best Western (Burnet), and James and Terry from The Vistas Apartments (Marble Falls). We also would like to show our appreciation to Sheriff Joe Pollock and the Burnet Police Department, and the generous families and individuals in the city of Marble Falls and Burnet who welcomed us with their love and support. In particular, we would like to thank Sharon and Stan Zimberg for their warm and friendly welcome and great assistance, also the Resident Services Coordinator, Jeanene Olson from the Texas Housing Foundation and Lyn Odom. We would like to give a warm thanks to Kathleen Paige Elliot for extending her home and hospitality to us once we landed in Marble Falls, and the River Cities Daily Tribune, The Picayune, the Highlander Newspaper, Terry Haecker of "The Word" at KLGO (Austin), KVUE News, Marble Falls Housing Authority, and First Baptist Church in Marble Falls.

Special thanks to Ed Necker, Administrator of First Baptist Church of Marble Falls; Warren Ryder at Marble Falls ISD; the administrators, staff, teachers, counselors, coaches, and students at Marble Falls and Burnet ISD; Mrs. Anna Colon of Associated Catholic Charities; Mrs. Liz Zarsky of St. Vincent DePaul; Mrs. Patti Bougher from the Community Resource Center of Marble Falls; Debbie and Stan Cox of Haynes Printing, Shane Stewart of State Farm, and Boulder Creek Ministries; Big thanks to Mr. & Mrs. Teeples and praise God for answered prayers for the property. We also would like to thank Kaboom for the kids' playground. Also, we would like to thank Luther Harrison of Samaritan's Purse, Ernest Sietz, all employers of SFJM families, the city of Austin, and San Antonio for giving us free tickets to allow our kids to enjoy a day at Six Flags; customers of The Real New Orleans Style Restaurants; the Red Cross and Salvation Army; FEMA and SBA; and local and state agencies.

In addition, we would like to give a big thanks to our church member, Courtnaye Richard who sifted through each transcript and transformed its verbal content into a written format with spiritual insight, guidance, and creativity. Also, we would like to extend special thanks to Alicia Villanueva at Advanced Editing in Austin, who made the final edits with her expertise to improve the overall manuscript unto completion. And we would like to give thanks to Author House Publishing for their patience and professionalism in getting our story published. Lastly, we would like to thank *our* new governor Rick Perry for governing the awesome outpouring of hospitality throughout the great state of Texas!

WARNING!!!
THERE'S A STORM COMING!

"In 1995, I had a dream that I was walking on top of water. There was muddy brown water everywhere; businesses, homes, and cars were all underwater. And when I woke up, I said, 'Wow, New Orleans was underwater.'"

~ Juanita Fraise

"Three months before Hurricane Katrina hit, I had a dream that there was this great flood and the Superdome cracked open. The Lord told me to run to higher ground. And when I got on the rooftop of this tall building, I looked down and yelled to the people walking on the streets, 'The water is coming! Danger! Danger!' But nobody listened. They just kept walking by. Then suddenly, the water came rushing in, and they were all washed away."

~ Viola Chapman

"In early July of 2005 while my family and I were on vacation in Florida, I had a vision…a vision that the city of New Orleans would be washed away, and everyone in it would have to leave in order to rebuild it. I thought, 'That would never happen.' Little did I know that God had just given me a glimpse of what was to come! In just one month, my vision had come to pass. Hurricane Katrina made landfall in New Orleans as a dangerous Category Three hurricane, and eventually, everyone had to leave the city. Several months later, people began working on rebuilding New Orleans. Hurricane Katrina was noted to be one of the most devastating natural disasters in American history."

~ Courtnaye Richard

"We were living with my parents waiting to buy a house, but we couldn't at the time because of our financial state. So we decided to rent an apartment in eastern New Orleans to be closer to the church. Well, the apartment complex had three levels, and the apartment for rent was on the second floor. We weren't sure, plus the rent was too high. We talked to our pastor to get some direction regarding whether or not we should rent it or keep looking. He told us to get it anyway because God was going to make a way for us, and then he added, 'This way, you will be away from the high water that's coming.' We obeyed. And thank God we did, because when Katrina struck, our apartment was barely touched, yet the bottom and top levels were utterly destroyed."

~ Minister Tara Griffin

"One Tuesday night at women's Bible Study in July 2005, the Lord spoke to me to give a message of warning, but I was too afraid to say it. I was only ten years old at the time, and I told my mom that I couldn't get the words out of my mouth. So she told me to write it down, and this is what God said, 'Chance after chance I have given you, and you have disobeyed Me! I will send a storm to take away all of your stuff!'"

~ Jeanecia Edwards

INTRODUCTION

"Ye have seen what I did unto the Egyptians, and how I bare
you on eagles' wings, and brought you unto Myself."
Exodus 19:4

I'll never forget the message I preached one Wednesday night in January 2005 to my congregation, Smoking for Jesus Ministry, located in Eastern New Orleans, Louisiana...

"You know, New Orleans could be twenty feet under water in no time with just *one* storm – just one! Imagine, in one day, life as we know it could all change in a matter of hours, minutes, even seconds. Think about that for a moment. I mean, if we take a look around and see all of these things that are happening right now in the world with the tragic events and current weather patterns...with the tsunami that wiped out and killed over 180,000 people in minutes, not to mention the tornadoes and earthquakes we are seeing around the world.

"Man, we just don't understand. I believe that God has bestowed tremendous grace and mercy on America. But unfortunately, it seems as though some of us are very dull when it comes down to spiritual things. Sometimes it takes an awaking like 9/11 and the tsunami to really understand what God is doing and how close we are to the end of the world right now. Whether people want to believe it or not, God is moving and shaking things up to get our attention and to prepare us for the soon return of His Son

Jesus Christ. And if you notice, when God allows things like this to happen, there is absolutely nothing that we can do to stop it."

At that time, Hurricane Katrina wasn't even a thought in my mind. I was simply speaking what God was giving me. Yet, I believe that God uses us, His people, to predict certain things that He is going to do in the future. And He gives us the authority to speak it. To some of us, God gives dreams and visions, and to others, He speaks directly. But there is a catch, literally. Once the message goes forth, it is up to us to listen, grab hold, and take heed of its teachings or warnings. God wants His people to experience true salvation today, not tomorrow, because no one is promised another day. I believe He used Hurricane Katrina as another wake up call for those who were still sleeping. And for others, it was a test of faith.

Without a doubt, Hurricane Katrina was predicted to be DEADLY! Although we heard the warnings, as a city, a people, a church, and even as a pastor, we did not have a clue as to the true magnitude of her power. Nor could we imagine how she would impact our lives or reshape our future. However, if there was anyone, and I do mean absolutely anyone who knew exactly what we were about to face…it was *God.*

He had a plan. He always has a plan, no matter how bad the situations look. In Jeremiah 29:11 (NIV), He reveals, "'For I know the plans I have for you,' declares the Lord, 'plans to prosper you and not to harm you, plans to give you hope and a future.'" Sometimes, I admit that it is not always easy to wait on God to reveal His plans to us, and sometimes even harder to understand them…especially when things look grim, dark, and uncertain. But we can rest assure and trust that He is always going to do what is best for us in the end, regardless of what we may have to go through in this life. And we can relax in the fact that there is nothing that is ever going to happen without His knowing, because He sits high and looks down low upon the earth.

I truly believe that the Spirit of God swept through that Wednesday night Bible study back in 2005 simply to warn us that Hurricane Katrina was coming. Being human, we thought perhaps it would not happen, or maybe we would not be there when it did occur. I spoke the words without realizing that this prophecy would truly come to pass right before my very eyes and in my lifetime. This event showed me that although we really do not know *when* God is going to move or do something big, we know that He *will* do it, eventually. It makes me think of how it will be when Jesus comes back – He will come like a thief in the night, with the obvious signs being right upon us. And I honestly believe that it will happen in our lifetime. That is why we have to make sure that we are in right standing with God every day.

Some people may ask, "Why now? Why release this book today?" The reason is because I believe that God placed this book on my heart and that He commissioned me to help people understand what He is doing through the hurricanes, floods, tornadoes, earthquakes, tsunamis, wars, and devastations of life right now.

The point is that these things are actually meant to wake us up while there is still time. The Bible tells us that when we begin to see these things happening within the earth, we should know that this is only the beginning of sorrow (Mark 13:8). So there is more to come. God is crying out, "Believe, repent, confess and turn away from your sins, and come to Me. I love you and I want a relationship with you. My Son is coming back soon. So live for Me and deny yourself. I want you to trust and have faith in Me. For the end is near! Repent…before it is too late!"

Furthermore, I believe that He's speaking through the storms that strike our lives, such as divorce, broken relationships, loss of loved ones, job layoffs, foreclosures, financial hardships, diseases, and the list goes on. Without a doubt, God loves us all very much and He wants nothing more than for us to live in peace and have life more abundantly on the earth. But life on earth is not all He wants us to be striving towards. Instead, He wants us to set our affections on things above and not on things of the earth (Colossians 3:2). It's about eternal life in heaven.

Please listen. This is not just another story about Hurricanes Katrina and Rita, but an extraordinary one that I can only imagine will change the way you think about the storms of life forever. God wants you to get something out of this book that will not only help you, but also your family, friends, coworkers, and church family to understand what He is doing in the world today. It is not by chance that you picked up this book. God has you on His mind and on His heart…daily.

As you read, you will find that this book is composed of multiple testimonies of how God started one church that was originally from New Orleans on a journey through a modern day wilderness after the storms, and how He took us from one level of faith to the next.

By far, Hurricane Katrina was not a mistake, nor was it caused by the devil or Mother Nature as some individuals have stated in the past. Rather, it was a mighty move of God. He shook the foundations of His people on the Mississippi Gulf coast and touched the lives of thousands across the world through this storm. God allowed it to happen to draw men, women, teenagers, and children to repentance and unto Himself…and if you take a look back at the reports, many turned to the Lord for salvation, strength, peace, and hope in such a devastating time in American history.

As you peel through each page, I challenge you to go through this journey of tragedy, faith, hope, and love, and in the process, examine your life to see what God is trying to tell *you* through your own storms.

But in the meantime…*Mount Up!* And get ready for a journey that you will never forget. This is the story of *How One Church Survived Hurricanes Katrina and Rita*.

CHAPTER ONE:

The Calm before the Storm

New Orleans, Louisiana

"You will keep in perfect peace all who trust in You,
all whose thoughts are fixed on You!"
Isaiah 26:3 NLT

O n Friday, August 26, 2005 the weather was beautiful and the
afternoon winds were calm. Children returning home from school
were anticipating the freedom of the weekend and my wife Claudette and I
were looking forward to a few days of much needed rest. We'd just returned
home from Destin, Florida after conducting our annual Marriage Refresher
for the married couples of our church *Smoking for Jesus Ministry*, where I
am the pastor. However, while getting settled back in, I turned on the local
news only to learn that a potentially catastrophic Category Five hurricane
named Katrina was threatening to strike our city within 72 hours. The
city, though, didn't seem to be too concerned. There was no uproar or sign
of panic. Oh, had we only known what was to come. I look back now a bit
wistfully at how calm we all were, before the storm.

At the time, our church was located in eastern New Orleans and
had been in operation since 1996. We had regularly scheduled weekly
services such as Monday night Bible Studies, Tuesday women's Bible study,
Wednesday night discipleship class, Saturday corporate prayer, and Sunday

morning services. We were also in the process of building a new church adjacent to our current structure. That weekend, though, our plans were in for a drastic change.

At 6:00 a.m. Saturday morning, I turned on the television to hear the meteorologist report that Hurricane Katrina was looking more and more like she was headed directly for our city. My initial thought was, "Perhaps she may turn and miss us." In the past, we'd evacuated for several other storms, but nothing had ever happened. And to be honest, I didn't really feel like running from another hurricane. I was exhausted from our trip, and simply wanted to recuperate before getting back into my normal routine.

For a moment, I seriously considered hunkering down and weathering it out. After hearing later weather reports, though, I knew that I needed to make a decision soon, because time was running out. Based on what it looked like, we were up against a pretty intense and potentially deadly storm. I began to pray and seek God for direction, asking, "Lord, what should we do? Should we stay or should we go?" And shortly thereafter, all signs pointed to "Pack up and EVACUATE!"

*   *   *

On the afternoon of Saturday, August 27, Mayor Ray Nagin and other state officials began reporting that people needed to start seriously making plans to evacuate the city, because a mandatory evacuation would be ordered on Sunday. Some New Orleanians were already packed and ready to go. Others had decided to get an early start on traffic and were already rolling. As I watched on television, I could see that the highways were beginning to fill. I knew then that we needed to create an immediate evacuation plan. That's when I told my wife to get on the phone and call Minister June Roth, our church event coordinator, to assist with the planning.

Minister June got on it right away, and she reminded me and my wife about the Emmanuel Fletcher Retreat Center in Lumberton, Texas. Our church had made plans to stay there for our annual family retreat later on that year. So that worked out perfectly. Minister June called the owners and worked out all the details, then let us know that the retreat center was preparing for our arrival. That was good news.

After that, I asked her to use the church directory to contact all of our members to see who might need a place to stay, and to create a list of those who would evacuate with us to the center. I also told her to ask church members if they knew of anyone else – their family or friends – who might also come with us. Even though the retreat center was not free, we were not at all concerned about the cost. We would take care of that later. We were more concerned about people making it out alright.

Minister June informed everyone who was coming to bring three days worth of clothing, medical records, and important documents, just as suggested by our mayor, and she let them know that we would all meet up at the church Sunday morning at 8:00 a.m.

* * *

When I woke up early Sunday morning on August 28 and turned on the television, I quickly discovered that Hurricane Katrina had not budged and was still on her predicted path to strike our city within 24 hours. She was headed towards us and the forecast revealed that we could experience a storm surge from Lake Ponchartrain about 18 feet high with seven foot waves above the surge! My wife, who was watching the news with me, turned to me and said, "I knew this was not going to be a regular Sunday morning."

Usually around 7:30 a.m., I would see the sanctuary filling up with church members and visitors dressed in their Sunday best, parents dropping their crying infants off at the nursery, and children and youth scurrying off to their Sunday school classes. An hour later, the Praise Team would be singing praise and worship songs, our announcement team would be reading off the clipboard of important events, and shortly thereafter I would be preaching the Word of God. But on that particular Sunday, God had another plan. We were preparing to evacuate.

I'll never forget that day. When I looked around the sanctuary, everyone was dressed comfortably in jeans, shorts, t-shirts, and tennis shoes, including me and my wife. We wanted to be comfortable for the journey ahead. There was no time to waste, so I informed everyone of the upcoming plans and the route that we were going to take, and then I proceeded with this prayer:

"Lord, we thank You and we honor You once again. Father, we thank You for the storm that You are sending our way. In Your Word, You said to give thanks in all things, because this is Your will concerning us in Your Son Christ Jesus. God, we know that You work everything out and You do all things for the good of Your people. So we are not complaining this morning, Lord. We just ask to hear Your Spirit and to be able to flow accordingly. Master God, now we ask that You watch over and protect each one of us and guide us on the road. We look forward to returning to see Your miracle in this place, no matter how high the winds get or what may blow away.

"You said that we have a foundation with You, and that we can count on You. So we expect when we come back, we will see Your mighty hand move again in this city. And O God, even with the tragedy that You may bring upon this city, perhaps some will repent Lord, and some may want to give their lives over to You, Father. We know very well that some people may lose their lives. Perhaps it may cause those who are still alive to want to serve You, Lord, and not the world. So Father, have Your way in this city. Help us to submit to Your will, Father, and have us do whatever You want us to do today. Help us to be obedient to Your voice. We thank You that You have provided us a place of refuge. Some do not have money, Lord, and some do not have ways to get out. But we thank You for giving us a place and a way of escape. Now please guide us with wings of eagles, Lord. We thank You, Father. In the name of Jesus, Amen."

* * *

As we proceeded out of the church, we were pretty calm and in good spirits. Although we took it seriously, most were thinking of the many times that we'd evacuated in the past, only to find that it was either a scare or resulted in little to no damage. So many of us figured it would be just like the other times. And most members were looking forward to a nice break away from work and school for a few days.

I remember seeing members' cars and trucks packed to full capacity with pillows, blankets, games, food, soft drinks, CDs, and DVDs for the long ride. For most of them, this was something fun! It was like they were going on a three-day vacation. It was just another road trip.

Around 9:30 a.m., those of us in our vehicles overheard the radio announcer say that Mayor Ray Nagin had just issued a citywide mandatory evacuation! Nothing like it had ever happened before. The news reports shifted from relaxed citizens of New Orleans to families hurriedly boarding up their homes and filling their vehicles with water, food, luggage, and gas. And the highways were getting more and more congested by the minute.

After we received that report, I knew that we needed to get moving. By 10:00 a.m., the caravan headed out onto Chef Menteur Highway towards I-10. However, while my wife left with the caravan, I, and a few other brothers from the church stayed behind to finish boarding up the properties. Elder William Tumblin who has been in the ministry alongside me for over twenty years, helped orchestrate this part of the process. This is what he remembers:

Elder William

> "After we prayed, I, Pastor Monnet, and a few other men stayed behind to help board up our church, administrative building, restaurant, hair salon, nursery, and our pastor's house. We also boarded up the House of Joseph and the House of Leah, which were homes for both single men and women. Once we were done with that, we didn't waste any time. We knew the storm was coming. So the next step was to get into our vehicles and hit the highway."

We quickly realized that we would not be able to get out of the city the usual way. Those who are familiar with running from hurricanes know that sometimes you have to take back roads and highways that you normally would not travel to avoid just sitting there for hours in gridlock traffic. So once my wife informed us that the traffic was really bad on I-10 headed west, the men and I then headed out in another direction towards Slidell, which was going east. We figured that going the back way would be a little less congested, which, unfortunately, wasn't the case. We took Highway 90, which brought us to Baton Rouge in about five hours. Usually, it only takes 45 minutes to get there. Reports later showed that it took some people *nine* hours just to reach that distance.

Let me just say that it was total turmoil getting out of the city and out of harm's way. There were a lot of people on the roads. Traffic was literally bumper to bumper the whole time while driving to Lumberton, Texas. I remember while me and the brothers were on the road, I looked over into the cars beside me and could see the weariness and fatigue on people's faces. There was a sense of heaviness in the atmosphere. Every gas station was packed with cars, trucks, and vans, and soon, some of the stations were completely wiped out of gas. Men, women, and children stood in long lines waiting to use the restrooms gas station after gas station. It was real. It was really real. None of us had ever seen or experienced anything like it before in our lives, including my wife, who recalls:

Wife Claudette

"When we got to Kenner, which is normally about a twenty minute drive from eastern New Orleans, the traffic was backed up for so many miles. It took us about four hours to get there. There were scores of cars that were bumper to bumper. Everyone was moving so slow. We were leery of getting off the roads because we were concerned that it would take us hours to get back on. But we had to stop numerous times, because we had to consider the fact that we had kids, teenagers, and elderly members with us. So we had to get off at different intersections. [When we'd stop,] I could hear people saying, 'We're going through all of this and this storm is probably not going to do anything.' A lot of people were getting edgy, even some of our members. This wasn't a normal situation. But everybody stayed cool. We just talked to each other and encouraged one another to keep pressing. I remember listening to Marvin Sapp's song, 'Do You Know Him?' It made me think about our situation. It was like, 'Did we really know Jesus?' It was as if God was testing us to see if we were going to act like true Christians. There were people cutting in the bathroom lines, cussing all around us, and some of them had really bad attitudes. This was a time to really put our faith into

action, show the love and character of Christ, and believe
that God was going to get us through this ordeal."

It was much different from past hurricane evacuations. Actually, it was worse. It seemed like more people were trying to flee this one. But I could totally understand why because of the severity and size of Hurricane Katrina. She was predicted to hit us head on as a Category Four or Five hurricane, and she was scheduled to strike New Orleans early Monday morning. So there was much pandemonium within the city!

Although all of this was happening around us, God filled me with His peace, and I didn't really worry about what would happen. Even though I had no idea what we would encounter in the next few days, I believed that God was with us. Plus, I didn't really think that the prophecy God had given me was going to come to pass yet! Little did I know. Thank God, though, for His peace and for the knowledge that we would make it through, no matter the weather.

CHAPTER TWO:

In the Midst of the Storm

Lumberton, Texas

*"So if you are suffering in a manner that pleases God,
keep on doing what is right, and trust your lives to the
God who created you, for He will never fail you."*
1 Peter 4:19 NLT

On Sunday, August 28 around 11:00 p.m., my wife's caravan pulled into the parking lot of the Emanuel Fletcher Church Alive and Conference and Retreat Center in Lumberton, Texas. Normally, it would've taken four hours to get there; that day, it took twelve. Imagine that! My wife recalls the journey:

Wife Claudette

"It was indeed a long trip. When we got there, we were literally exhausted. But the owners and staff of the retreat center welcomed us with open arms and treated us with such kindness. They even prepared a hot meal upon our arrival. I remember seeing everyone – men, women, and children – hurrying off to the cafeteria to grab something to eat. By that time, we'd worked up a pretty good appetite.

We were so grateful for their spontaneous hospitality. Before dinner was over, Minister June and I worked on a plan for sleeping arrangements. There was a two-story dormitory style building, with showers, huge bathrooms, a wash room, kitchen, library, guest lounge, and classrooms. There was also a guest house on site to accommodate individuals with special needs, and it had a suite for me and my husband to occupy, which was quite homey."

According to my wife, the place seemed pretty accommodating for all of us. However, first things first, everybody needed to get some rest from the extended road trip. So Minister June helped with the room assignments:

Minister June

"I was placed in charge to help coordinate room arrangements. I have this natural drive to help others in need, so as exhausted as I was at the time, I immediately jumped into my role, grabbed the clipboard, and was off running like the Energizer Bunny! My adrenaline was supernaturally pumping, because God knew that in my own strength I was too tired and weak to do it all. Everyone needed a bed to sleep in, so it was my job to orchestrate this process. The retreat center was a dormitory style setting with many beds, but not a lot of rooms. Consequently, I had to do room assignments for men, women, children, and teenagers. The Lord gave me instantaneous insight! And trust me, I needed it. Minister Monnet (pastor's wife) and I arranged for the single women to board together on the first floor, while the men and teenage boys resided upstairs. The women with children slept downstairs, and unfortunately, the married couples were unable to stay together due to limited spacing. I was married myself, so that was kind of a shock at first,

but considering the circumstances, no one complained. We
all figured it would only be for a couple of days anyway."

When I arrived around 2:00 a.m. Monday morning with some of the
brothers who'd traveled with me, we discovered that everyone was already
settled and asleep in their beds. So we followed suit behind them to get
some sleep ourselves. I knew that it was only a matter of hours before
Hurricane Katrina would make landfall in the city of New Orleans.

*   *   *

In the morning, the kids occupied their time by playing outdoors, while
the youth hung out with one another, and the adults just kind of sat around
waiting to get word on what was happening in the city. I couldn't help but
think about times in the past when we'd evacuated only to discover that it
was just another scare, and if that were the case this time, we'd soon be back
on the road returning home to our normal everyday lives.

That evening, things were pretty quiet. On Tuesday, we listened to
reporters say that there had been only minor damage, just a few power
lines down, and that they thought New Orleans had missed the brunt of
the storm. Joyfully, we all thought we were home free.

But on early Wednesday morning, things changed dramatically. As we
watched the big screen TV in the center's mid-sized lounge, we heard the
reporters tell a completely different story. Something had happened that
many New Orleanians had only imagined and always feared: the levees had
broken!

We learned that not just one or two, but *three* levees had been breached
in various parts of the city. The 17th Street Canal, the Industrial Canal,
and the London Avenue Canal floodwall had fallen. Water was pouring
into the city. At that point, we knew there was a grim possibility that, best
case scenario, thousands of citizens of New Orleans were now homeless,
or, worst case scenario, left behind for dead. Within minutes of turning the
TV on, the lounge swelled with church members rushing in to see what was
happening to our city.

One of our elder members, Juanita Fraise, remembers something quite
similar happening with Hurricane Betsy back on September 9, 1965:

Juanita

"After seeing what was happening with Hurricane Katrina on television, my mind quickly went back to when Hurricane Betsy came through New Orleans and the levees broke by Florida Avenue in the Lower Ninth Ward and on both sides of the Industrial Canal. Those flood waters had people on roof tops trying to get out, but unfortunately, some didn't make it out alive. I remember one of my friends telling me that he witnessed one of his neighbors lose nine children when the water from the levees came rushing in. He watched them one by one plunge into the water and die. That was terrible. But many knew the storm was coming. I guess they just didn't heed the warnings. I evacuated when the city officials sounded the alarm to get out. As a result, my life was saved. Thank God! Unfortunately, many other lives were taken and homes were destroyed. It was a very sad reality. It was almost like back in the days of Noah when he tried to warn the people that the flood was coming and they thought he was crazy. They were having their parties, eating and drinking their fill, and laughing. They never thought it would happen. Then one day, it literally poured, and they were destroyed. If only they would have listened. So when I heard Hurricane Katrina was coming, I wasn't taking any chances. When my pastor said that the church was making plans to evacuate to get out of the city, I was on board. And after watching the news and seeing the devastation with Katrina, I couldn't believe what I was witnessing *again*. It was too hard to see it happening for a second time. But this time, it was *worse*. Three levees had broken! There were so many people who had stayed behind. I couldn't understand. They were warned. I needed to stay prayerful, because I still had my four adult children who'd decided to stay behind. It was only by the grace of God that my church family was able to get out in time."

We were so thankful that we didn't try to weather this one out. As one report after another rained in and revealed the utter devastation, we were baffled. My daughter, Feandrell Brown, expresses what she felt after seeing the destruction:

Feandrell

"When I first saw what was happening to our city, I was at a loss for words. I didn't know whether to cry or stand in shock. I felt like I'd been struck by two storms, because right before the evacuation for Hurricane Katrina, I had just lost my marriage of 12 years to a bitter divorce. But of course, after watching the news I realized that I'd then probably lost my house, clothes, all of my possessions, and my job at the church's beauty salon. So at that moment, I felt like I'd lost everything. It hit me all at once. I felt so alone. And even though I had my three children, sisters, church members, and my dad and mom (who are the pastor and lady elect of the church), I *still* felt alone. I knew God was there, because He said that He would never leave me nor forsake me, but for a moment I was struck with an overwhelming sense of loneliness. And then the Lord reminded me of Isaiah 40:31, 'They that wait upon the Lord shall renew their strength, they shall mount up with wings as eagles; they shall run, and not be weary; and they shall walk, and not faint.' In that instant, I knew that God was telling me that if I trusted and waited on Him, that He was going renew my strength in every way imaginable and carry me through it all. And I held onto that. I also remembered something my mother had told me before the storm hit: 'God is going to change your situation one way or another.' At the time, I didn't know what she meant exactly or how He would do it, but after watching the news that day and recalling that familiar Scripture, I had a feeling that change was suddenly beginning to take place in my

life, and that God was in the process of giving me a fresh
start. I just had no idea that it would take a devastating
Category Three hurricane to reconstruct my life."

That was a pretty rough time for our daughter. She had just recently
come back to the church after being gone for three years. But the Lord saw
fit to bring her back to us a year prior to Hurricane Katrina's arrival. As a
result, she and our three grandchildren were able to make the trip with all
of us. Boy, she was hanging on to our coattails like a newborn baby. Only
this time, she was not letting go. And little did she know God was working
mysteriously on her behalf, just as He was doing with the rest of us.

* * *

By late Wednesday, August 31, 2005, news reports were saying that
New Orleans was eighty percent underwater. It was unbelievable! We
watched, devastated, as we saw a huge body of water engulfing a familiar
street sign at St. Bernard and Claiborne Avenue. The street pole was covered
with water, leaving only the green and white text of the sign exposed. And
that wasn't all. It was almost surreal watching cars and trucks float past the
tops of houses; it felt like we were watching a movie, not real life. When we
saw the bodies, though, countless, lifeless, floating in the waters on our once
dry city streets, we couldn't pretend like it was a film anymore. Everyone felt
so connected to those we saw on the news that those lifeless bodies became
our own, just for the moment.

The next few hours were understandably intense. We scrambled to get
a hold of family members and friends still in the city, but our calls didn't
connect. *Everyone* was trying to get in touch with people in the path of the
hurricane, and the phone companies just couldn't handle the high volume
of calls. I wasn't able to get in touch with my own four adult boys. Brenda
Woods gives her take on this wild experience:

Brenda

"The cell phones weren't working with the 504 area code.
No one was really able to get in touch with anyone. We kept

hearing, 'All circuits are busy.' I was really concerned about my brother. I didn't know where he was at the time, and after seeing everything that was happening on television with those who were left behind for dead in nursing homes, and those who had decided to weather it out being found trapped inside flooded homes yelling for help – I simply couldn't keep watching. It was too hard. It was unbelievable that something like this was actually happening in our city. I had prayed for years for a way to escape the dangers and violence of the city, but I had no idea that it would come in the form of a tragedy such as this one. All I could do was pray and thank God for delivering us at just the right time."

Praise God! We were very grateful that we had heeded the warnings and quickening from the Holy Spirit to evacuate while we still had a chance. The news stations were reporting that the thousands of people who had taken shelter in their homes, hotels, the New Orleans Superdome, and the Morial Convention Center were without power, water, and food. Many elderly who were sick were without medicine. Babies were without milk and children were crying from hunger. Due to the high water levels, it could be not just hours, reporters said, but possibly even days before help could arrive. We kept remembering and praying for people we knew who had stayed behind. My daughter Feandrell explains what was running through her mind, as does my nephew Dedrick Thompson:

Feandrell

"In the midst of everything that was happening in my own life, I was very concerned for my neighbor who'd told me that she was going to stay in her house and weather the storm with her three children. I didn't know what to expect. I was really praying for their safety. I could only imagine what they were going through at that time."

15

Dedrick

> "When they were showing people trapped in the Superdome, I was like, 'What! Trapped in the Superdome?' I figured if there were thousands of people trapped in the Superdome, then what was happening to the rest of New Orleans? And that's when I saw all of the water engulfing various parts of the city. Immediately, I thought to myself, we are *not* going back. It's over!"

Our mayor estimated that approximately one million people from New Orleans and the surrounding areas fled Hurricane Katrina's wrath. But even though this significant amount left, over 100,000 people didn't evacuate. About 20,000 took shelter at the Superdome, where, as we saw on the news, a large portion of its rooftop was literally ripped off due to intense winds, and rain began pouring inside. If our greatest buildings couldn't stand up to the storm, we could only imagine the fate of those who had chosen to stay in their own homes.

It was hard for us to watch because there was nothing we could do physically to help. We were miles away, and at the time, no one was able to get into the city. For awhile, we were unable to get in touch with one of our own members, Johnny Williams, who had decided to stay behind to weather it out. When he finally got through by phone, he recounted what had happened to him during the storm. Here is his story:

Johnny

> "The wind was strong and the rain was beating up against the window pane like a ravished beast. It was like Godzilla was pushing the house down. I never really understood the impact of a dangerous Category Three hurricane until I actually found myself living through one. I can't lie — immediately, fear gripped me. But then almost instantly, my faith in the Lord kicked in, which allowed me to trust Him. I admit there were times when the enemy, Satan, tried

to detour my thoughts from trusting God by telling me, 'You're not going to make it out of here alive. You're going to die. You're going to drown.' That's when I remembered the Scripture Isaiah 59:19 which reads, 'When the enemy shall come in like a flood, the Spirit of the Lord shall lift up a standard against him.' That was my lifeline. I had to stand on the sure foundation of my faith that Jesus Christ was going to see me through, and He did."

Johnny eventually got a ride to meet back up with us in Lumberton. We were, and are, so thankful that God spared his life.

*   *   *

The next several days went by in a blur. People were still hurting in New Orleans and dying of starvation and sickness. We heard that it was like a third world country down there. Desmond Green, who is now a member of our church, recalls his experience while waiting at the New Orleans Convention Center for help:

Desmond

"I was one who'd stayed behind as well to weather the storm. I didn't listen to the warning signs, because I thought it would be just like all the other evacuations. But when the water level began to rise and pour inside of my house, I had to bust through the attic to stay alive. I was trying to drown out the possibility that I might die up there by smoking cigarettes and drinking a bunch of alcohol. But after my high came down, I said, "Lord, if You get me out this alive, I'll stop drinking, smoking, cursing, running around with women, all of that.' I didn't know what else to do. My dad was a pastor, so I knew how to pray. And eventually, the water stopped rising and I was able to escape from the attic and go to the Convention Center to wait for help. But when I got there, it was like a living nightmare! There were thousands of people everywhere, but no buses to pick us up. Many were hollering and screaming, sitting and sleeping in dirty clothes and feces for days...just waiting. People's hair wasn't combed, and there were hungry babies, men, women, and children inside and outside the center. There were a lot of tears from lack of food, water, and medicine, and from heat exhaustion. People were dying out there! It was like a third world country. It was really a sad moment in time. Eventually, buses did arrive. But I have to say, it was really tough experiencing such desperate and helpless conditions in America."

Man! Who would've known that was going to happen but God? Through this experience, Desmond became a changed man – a saved man. I'm sure he wasn't the only one.

*   *   *

In Lumberton, we had to bow our heads to pray for those in New Orleans, but also lift our hands to thank God for shielding, covering, and protecting us from the utter devastation of the storm. We were just so thankful that the Lord had delivered us in time. While we were in the midst of giving God praise, glory, and honor for His keeping power, local news reporters and writers arrived Wednesday evening to cover a story on us.

They came out to interview us, thinking they had a juicy story of the down-and-out New Orleanians. But to their surprise, when they walked into the retreat center's cafeteria, what they found was not all what they had expected. They found about 200 church members worshiping and praising God! We were singing praises and dancing because we were extremely grateful and thankful that God had spared our lives. He had provided a place of refuge for us in Lumberton. There was simply nothing we could do but rejoice. The Bible says in Romans 5:3-4 (NLT), "We can rejoice, too, when we run into problems and trials, for we know that they help us develop endurance. And endurance develops strength of character, and character strengthens our confident hope of salvation."

When they came to interview us, the reporters were so overcome by emotion that they themselves had to put down their cameras, pens, pads, and microphones and, for a few moments, just weep. They had expected to see overwhelming distress, and, instead, they saw hope. God had changed their story!

The Lord had delivered us! The Scripture says in Exodus 15:2 (NLT), "The Lord is my strength and my song; He has given me victory." There was nothing else we could do but give praises unto Him. We couldn't get down and out based upon what we saw transpiring on television. Sure, there were tears…but there were tears of joy in the midst of the sadness. It was bittersweet, because although we had escaped the destruction, there were still others in the city who were stranded and in need. We continually prayed for them, for protection, for shelter, and for the salvation of many through this event. But again, we felt truly blessed and thankful that God led us out of the city in time. The Bible says to "Give thanks in all circumstances, for this is God's will for you in Christ Jesus" (1 Thessalonians 5:18 NIV).

Not only did we give thanks, but we also remained steadfast in our faith in God during those critical times. The Bible says to walk by faith, and not by sight (2 Corinthians 5:7). And I must admit, our members were really good soldiers in faith. I would definitely say that they handled the crisis well because of the solid foundation of faith that each of them had established long before the storm.

I remember teaching messages on faith before Hurricane Katrina was even a thought in our minds. As the Word says in Hebrews 11:6, "But without faith it is impossible to please *him*; for he that cometh to God must believe that he is, and that he is a rewarder of them that diligently seek Him." We had to place our faith in God. I believe the Lord actually prepared us through those messages and the Scriptures, because even though we were going through something tremendous in the natural at the time, He had prepared us in the spiritual. And I believe faith is what held us together *in the midst of the storm.*

I prophesied earlier in 2005, that New Orleans could experience a hurricane so devastating that it could bring this city 20 feet underwater.

Above are pictures of the New Orleans Superdome. The whole top covering was nearly ripped off during Hurricane Katrina. Our city was reported to be about 80% underwater. Some of the houses were almost totally submerged.

CHAPTER THREE:

Shelter from the Rain

Lumberton, Texas

"Your flock found a dwelling place in it; You, O God, in
Your goodness did provide for the poor and needy."
Psalm 68:10 AMP

It wasn't long before our congregation had to discuss that we may have all lost everything in the storm: houses, clothes, cars, jobs, and life as we once knew it. And to think, we had believed we were only going to be away from home for three days. That simply proved that we are not in control of our lives. Things can change at any given moment.

As we watched national news reporters, we learned, after evacuating all of the major shelters in New Orleans, with the exception of city officials and law enforcement, the city was nearly empty. It was hard to believe that this was actually happening! It was almost unreal. Yet, many of us had sensed this would happen someday; we just hadn't known when. On top of that, we didn't know how long it would be before we could get back into the city to see the damage for ourselves. I figured it would be significantly bad, especially considering what we'd already seen on television.

Yet I knew God had a plan. Granted, I didn't know what it entailed, but I knew that *He* was still in control of the overall situation...because He had allowed it. I knew that He had a purpose for it all, and maybe one day it would eventually make sense. For the moment, I didn't understand what He was doing, but I just had to lean on Him, and kick my faith into overdrive, while believing that He would make a way for us.

And early in the morning on Thursday, September 1, He did exactly that! We were awakened by the sound of large trucks and other vehicles driving into the retreat center, and it turned out that they were there to deliver goods and services to us! God had made a way for us. The newspaper and local news channels had spread the word that about 200 people from New Orleans had taken shelter in their town, and the community wanted to help.

God showed us His amazing love through the outpouring of hospitality in the Hardin County community of Lumberton. We hadn't known anyone prior to our arrival, but that didn't matter. The support from the community was a sure example of God's love and concern for His people. The Bible says in 1 John 3:18, "My little children, let us not love in word, neither in tongue; but in deed and in truth." And that Scripture came to life before our very eyes through this community. One of our ministers remembers this experience very clearly:

Minister Doris

"I was the person assigned to oversee the different things coming into the retreat center, and I saw firsthand the blessings of God. There were Wal-Mart trucks and people from all over the community coming in to deliver stuff to us in abundance and overflow. We had to open up the gym to house all of the items. For hours and even days, it did not cease. There was so much that we barely had enough room to receive it all. We had to categorize everything. We had so much stuff that it looked like a warehouse or, like my pastor would say, a giant flea market full of clothes, shoes, toiletries, cleaning supplies, soap, brushes, combs, sheets, pillows, blankets, canned goods, food, and the list just goes on. God really put us in an awesome place. His Word was fulfilled right before our very eyes. He really provided for us. This caused my faith to be refreshed and to increase. It was through this experience that God helped me to trust Him a little bit more and to go a little bit further. This is something that I will never forget."

None of us will ever forget how God showed up right when we needed Him. Honestly, we didn't have a chance to *not* trust Him. He blessed us through the city officials, judges, councilmen, local pastors, school administrators, and a great majority of the community who came in wholeheartedly to extend help. It was just a blessing. We ate meals three times a day, including snacks. I guess that would explain the late night stomach aches that registered church nurse Anitra Torns and Viola Chapman, LPN, helped to ease. Anitra explains:

Anitra

"I have to say that God really provided for our needs, even as a nursing staff. Once people knew that there were nurses on board, there were medical professionals in the area bringing over Tylenol, Motrin, insulin, gas-aids, syringes, stitches, medical scissors, needles, tape, bandages, stuff to take care of splints; whatever we needed to do to take care of simple injuries or aches and pains, we had it. We had so many supplies and meds in abundance that we had to utilize one of the vacant rooms upstairs in the dorm to house everything and provide operational hours to receive treatment and medication. It was unbelievable how God made a way for us."

The Lord really provided. David Armour can attest to that as well:

David

"My wife had just given birth to twin girls right before Hurricane Katrina hit. So we were on the road with newborns, and that was hard. We left without much money, and once we saw the devastation, we just knew that we had lost everything back at home. We'd just had a baby shower before the storm, but we'd left much of it. So we didn't really have anything. But after the people within the local community found out that we were there with newborn twins, they came out from everywhere, giving us gift cards, strollers, car seats, clothes, food – you name it, they brought it. The Lord really took care of us out there and blessed us so much that we received four to five times over what we had from the previous baby shower. He showed us that He really does take care of His people in whatever state we're in. We were so thankful for everyone who came out to help us."

Our congregation was so overwhelmed with thanks to God for the outpouring of love displayed there. We really did have more than we needed. In Philippians 4:19, the Scripture says, "But my God shall supply all your need according to His riches in glory by Christ Jesus." And His Word did not come back void.

*   *   *

As the days went on, we realized that we were going to be there longer than expected. The broken levees had allowed a lot of water into New Orleans, and the roads that weren't waterlogged were blocked by broken trees and downed power lines. Of course, that meant there was no electricity as well. Again, we had only packed for three days and money was beginning to run low. We didn't know how long the retreat center would allow us to stay. Essentially, we were homeless. Of all things, I never would've thought that I'd be homeless in 2005.

In spite of the circumstances, I knew that God was still in control and had all power to continue providing shelter for us. God is good all the time, regardless to whether the sun is shining or it's pouring down raining in our lives. From past experiences and even recent times, I knew that the Lord was going to continue showing up and showing out in every situation. We just had to wait with expectancy and faith. And sure enough, while we waited, there was a ray of light in the midst of a dark hour. Many of us were finally able to connect with our loved ones. God is good all the time!

My sons called to tell me that they were okay. Members were talking to their family and friends again, so that was a relief. Nothing could take the place of finally hearing the voice of loved ones on the phone, discovering that they were indeed alive and well. We were so very fortunate. Sadly, there were some citizens of New Orleans who did not have the same privilege. Some lost grandparents, mothers, fathers, children, and other family members and friends in the storm. On the news, there were continual reports of deceased bodies floating in the waters, lying on bridges, and being discovered on sidewalks. It was very disheartening. Each piece of news seemed to be bad news. When it rains, we all discovered, it quite literally pours. Our hearts and prayers continued to go out to those individuals who'd lost loved ones during the storm and its aftermath.

We ourselves could empathize, because during our stay in Lumberton, one of our own church members, Catherine Smith (who had traveled with us during the evacuation process) passed away after a hard fight with endometrial cancer. Before her passing, she had actually considered staying and weathering out the storm, but her daughter and son-in-law Travonda and Darron Woods (church members also) convinced her to leave the city. She had agreed, and, through her pain, she'd traveled over twelve hours with her family and the church caravan without *one* complaint. We're talking stage-three cancer! Even during her suffering, she lived up to Philippians 2:14 (NLT): "Do everything without complaining and arguing." Surely we can all learn a lesson from this. With that being said, Travonda reflected back on the memories of her mother's final days:

Travonda

"Before cancer, my mother was the type of woman who always seemed to have everything under control. She was a defense attorney who could handle the toughest cases. But when this disease took over her life and the doctors told her that she only had six months to live, she soon realized that this was something she had absolutely no control over. Instead, she had to rely on God and me to help her through this trying and difficult time in her life. And during that time, I must say that my pastor and his wife really were there for us. While in Lumberton, Minister Monnet coordinated a team of women to help sit with my mom, pray, and help out around the clock. I really appreciated their love and support. I needed it, because this was one of the hardest things that I've ever had to experience, seeing my mom in that state. So while everyone else was going through the natural storm with Hurricane Katrina, I was going through my own personal one. But I knew that God had a bigger plan for it all, because I believe that He sent both storms to help me draw closer to my mom, husband, three children, and, most importantly, to Him. It made all of us realize just how much we need Him. I know this because, in my mom's final moments, I remember asking her, 'Mom, if there is anything in you that needs to make things right with the Lord, say His name.' She couldn't really talk or breathe much at that point in her illness, but through the strength of the Lord, she managed to give just a little bit more and called on the name of Jesus. Even to the end, she gave. Throughout her life, she was a giver. She would give even when she didn't really have it to give. She would just believe that God would take care of her if she took care of others. And she was right. But by far, I think the most important thing that she could have ever given was her life to Jesus Christ. And she did that long before she took her final breath that late night on September 16, 2005. Knowing this, God gave me the peace and strength that I needed to live on without her."

Yes, God does give us the necessary strength to live on when we lose our loved ones. I know this from experience as well. When I lost my mother and father, He was there to comfort me through His Divine Presence and His

Word. I hold onto my memories too, just as Travonda holds onto cherished thoughts of her mother. And we pray the same for others who lost their loved ones through Hurricane Katrina.

*   *   *

After a couple of weeks had gone by, we were finally able to get back into the city. So me and several brothers packed up a few things and prepared for our first trip to New Orleans – post Katrina. Not many people from the city were allowed to get back in. It was only by the favor of the Lord and His grace that we were able to enter. Granted, we were only allowed to stay for one day, but we were grateful.

We were informed by city officials that the environmental conditions were very unsafe at the time and that there were highly strict limitations in place on our time there, so we couldn't grab as much as we'd anticipated in such a short period of time. We weren't there just for our stuff, though; we also wanted to see for ourselves the effects of the hurricane.

We'd heard a lot about it and had watched a great deal of coverage on television, but now we were able to see the tragedy with our very own eyes. I'll tell you, it was a sad sight to see. As we drove into the city of New Orleans on I-10 going east, instantly our senses were awakened. Immediately after entering the city, we were greeted by the stench of old sewage and death.

As we continued to drive on the highway, we witnessed hundreds of cars piled up under bridges and trees split in half and turned upside down. As I looked over the cement rails of the interstate, I observed several more vehicles pinned against fences in neighborhoods, and waterlines as high as ten feet or more on the outside of homes.

But I think the most shocking and most surreal moment of the drive was when I caught a glimpse of the holes in the rooftops of homes where helpless New Orleanians had stood screaming and crying, waving white rags for help. I had watched these scenes on television, but now it was all too real.

And as we drove further, we discovered that it was like a warzone down there. Martial law was everywhere! There were certain points in the city that we couldn't cross, but others we could with an escort. And there were countless vacant homes, among those homes with white, spray paint to identify the deceased. These were individuals who unfortunately either could not get out in time, did not have means to escape, or who simply did not heed the warning signs to evacuate Hurricane Katrina's dangerous and destructive path. Our hearts and prayers went out to those who had lost their friends, neighbors, and loved ones.

*   *   *

Once we'd reached eastern New Orleans, we got a chance to briefly see the church and our homes. When I first walked into the church, it was unbelievable! Mud was everywhere. But thank God we were all wearing our big rain boots. We also had on layers of clothing (as instructed by city officials) and face masks to protect against the dangerous fumes and bacteria in the air. We had brought our own food and water because we knew that the water there wasn't good for drinking and there weren't many stores open to purchase food. So we went prepared.

When I looked around inside the church, I saw that it had been ransacked by the storm. Chairs had been thrown all over the sanctuary, trash was everywhere, and the dark black waterline stained the walls near the roof. Interestingly, in the midst of all the rubble, the wooden podium which I stood behind almost every Sunday was still positioned in its rightful place…unmoved. That was amazing!

After a day of seeing the devastation in the city and the church, it was time to go. I knew that there would be a lot of work that would need to be done in the future, but it was not at all the time then. As for that moment, there was only time enough to pack up and get back on the highway to return to Lumberton.

*   *   *

Once we were back in Lumberton and had reported on what we'd seen in New Orleans, we realized that we needed to just make do with where we were. Carol Smothers shares her story:

Carol

"Considering our circumstances, we had to make ourselves comfortable. We weren't going anywhere anytime soon.

And after spending a couple of weeks in the dorm with the women downstairs, I quickly began to realize that God had a plan to draw us closer together as a church. Over time, I really began to bond and get to know my sisters in Christ, and we had fun! Sometimes we would get together and go to the nearby Wal-Mart to help pass the time and get our minds off of what was happening around us. Other times, we'd just sit around and talk and share life stories and a few laughs. They found out that I had a sense of humor, and I discovered that some of them were crazy (in a good way). It's true that you never really know a person until you live with them. In spite of it all, I believed God knew what He was doing. He was showing us how to have true godly relationships and how to really care and look out for one another in sisterly love. For instance, when clothes would come in from the community, I remember having something on my bed that one of the sisters gave to me because she saw something in one of the bags or boxes that she thought I might like. That brought joy to my heart. Things like that really made the difference during such an uncertain time."

As Carol discovered, God continued to place blessings in our laps in the middle of our uncomfortable circumstances. One of the most memorable events I witnessed was when the brothers of the church came together to make things more comfortable for their families. Many of them had received gift cards from various charity organizations, so they ventured out and bought little televisions, refrigerators, and comforters for their rooms, and made sure that their wives and children had everything that they needed. The singles worked together to keep things afloat on their end. The men were getting jobs, and a few of the members were even applying for local community colleges. It was comforting to see them adapt to the situation at hand.

We needed to get back to a bit of normalcy. The kids had been out of school for a few weeks, so mothers began registering their children into the local schools. And the kids were naturally excited. Granted, it was a new environment for them and a little bit of a culture shock, because New Orleans is a predominantly black city and Lumberton, well, is not. But nonetheless, the kids woke up at 6:00 a.m. daily to welcome the big yellow school buses that drove them to their new schools, and I heard not one complaint.

I encouraged constructive and fun activities to help everyone to get their minds off of the tragedy. For instance, some married couples had picnics with one another, some members went to Wal-Mart to pass time, some read books, and others did hair, like beautician Tiffany Thomas:

Tiffany

"Once I found the hair store, it was on! Doing hair was therapeutic for me. It took my mind off of the situation. And the women who would sit in my chair expressed how getting their hair flat ironed, weaved, braided, curled, crimped, or straightened would numb the reality of what was happening around us. We would even sing praises together in the process. Hey! When you feel bad inside, you at least want to look good on the outside. So I would put on some praise and worship music and do hair. It's a girl thing! And it helped. It really did. God knows what we need when we need it most."

*   *   *

While I waited for some answers from the Lord as to what to do next, we still had church. We never stopped having church, actually. Wendy Amour recalls this:

Wendy

"Our pastor was still preaching in spite of what we were going through. He never stopped! I really saw his love for the Lord and for us during that time. He could've stopped and focused on his losses and personal situation, but instead there he was with all of us in a retreat center far away from home, making sure that we not only had natural food, but spiritual food as well. He was still preaching and teaching us the Word of God. Now that's faithfulness and dedication. I count it a privilege, because I know people who were less fortunate. For instance, some of my family members called me and were surprised that we'd traveled with our church and said, 'Ya'll pastor actually took ya'll with him? We can't find our pastor and his wife, neither the members.' It was like they were scattered sheep left without a shepherd. So I count it a blessing that he considered our well-being when he and his wife were evacuating. They could've figured out their own way, but instead, they took the time to make arrangements for us. He prepared as best as he could to accommodate everyone who was interested in taking shelter from the rain. He tried not to leave anyone behind without an offer. And as a result, most of us were together, in unity, as one church in the Lord. God made provision for all of us through our pastor. And for that I am forever grateful."

As a pastor, my members were entrusted to me before this all began. So it was not a time for me to lean on my own understanding. We all needed a word from the Lord to comfort us, reassure us, and keep us strong during that time. That's why I deemed it necessary for us to continue having Monday night men's Bible study, Wednesday night Bible study, and Sunday service at the retreat center's cafeteria. I couldn't stop preaching.

God knew what He was doing through the storm. He had a plan for all of it, even when I had not a clue as to what to do next. Sure, I had thoughts of maybe leasing or buying a church in the nearby area. Nothing was certain. At the time, we were sharing space and services with Church Alive (the retreat center's church), but I knew that wasn't going to work forever. I had to just keep praying and seeking the Lord for direction.

After awhile, some of my members would catch me in the hall and ask me, "Now what are we going to do?" I was honest with them all and told them that I was waiting on God to reveal what He wanted us to do. At that time, it seemed we were just to *wait*. If I knew anything, it was to not start complaining. Surely this was not the time to start acting like the Israelites. I wasn't trying to stay in one place for forty years. We needed to act right in our wilderness situation.

I really was comparing what we were going through with the experience of Moses and the Israelites when they escaped from Egypt. It was like we had escaped from New Orleans, from all of the poverty, crime, and corruption, just as the Israelites had escaped from their bondage of slavery. So I knew how important it was to try to stay in the attitude of Christ during that time without murmuring or complaining. I didn't want any of us to forfeit whatever blessings God had in store for us in the future. That's why I remained prayerful. I knew that God would continue to lead and direct me, just as He had done in Moses' day.

* * *

Everyone was looking to me, the pastor, for direction, and honestly I did not have all the answers. I had to seek the Lord daily for wisdom and guidance. Again, I was just praying and waiting for something – a dream, a vision, a sign – but there was nothing for weeks. I had men, women, and children under my care that I had to look after and I needed God's direction. But it was like God was saying, "Are you going to trust Me without the dreams and without the visions?" I had to keep telling myself, "Just keep trusting Him. Just keep believing. He'll come through." And I knew that if I did that, then eventually, He would grant me direction for His people.

After three weeks of praying and seeking God, the direction finally came. At last, it was here! But I had no idea that it would come in the form of another Category Four hurricane. This time, her name was Rita, and her outer bands were larger than Hurricane Katrina's. But that wasn't the clincher. Are you ready for this? She was headed to none other than...the state of Texas. But wait, there's more! Her projected path was just miles away from where we were located.

Man, when I said that I didn't have a clue as to how God would move us, I really didn't have a clue. But after seeing Rita's intended path, all I could do was receive God's long awaited answer to my prayers: "EVACUATE AGAIN!"

This was our church owned
and operated establishment,
*The Smokehouse
Restaurant.*

After Hurricane Katrina's strong winds blew through New Orleans
on Aug. 29, the restaurant was destroyed. The winds left a gaping
hole on the exterior side of the building, where looters nearly stole
everything inside.

This was From Glory to Glory Beauty and Hair Salon. We almost lost everything inside the building. We were able to salvage the chair. Below is the front entrance of our church on Chef Mentuer Highway and the chairs are thrown all over the sanctuary, yet the tan podium never moved.

The city was crushed! It would take years to rebuild.

This was our home in eastern New Orleans. The water rose to approximately eight feet, almost reaching the ceiling which caused major loss and damage.

As we drove through the city, we saw many hand-written spray-painted signs on homes, pavement, rooftops, and even on this white refrigerator that stood on a desolate neighborhood street corner.

Above is a picture of the retreat center's cafeteria in Lumberton, Texas. We realized that we would not be returning home any time soon. So we continued to fellowship with one another, worship God, all the while sharing the facility with Pastor Richard Vaughn of Church Alive until the Lord gave me provision to move onward in our journey.

CHAPTER FOUR:

Uncharted Waters

Lone Star, Texas

"These trials are only to test your faith, to show that it is strong and
pure. It is being tested as fire tests and purifies gold – and your faith is
far more precious to God than mere gold. So if your faith remains strong
after being tried by fiery trials, it will bring you much praise and glory
and honor on the day when Jesus Christ is revealed to the whole world."

1 Peter 1:7 NLT

Hurricane Rita was coming! And you'd better believe that we were
watching her very closely. By all predictions, she was expected to
be bigger than Hurricane Katrina, and she was packing 140-mph winds
headed straight for the Beaumont and Port Arthur area. We were only
11 miles away. On Thursday, September 22, city and state officials began
announcing that people should evacuate Houston, Beaumont, and the
surrounding areas. For some areas, evacuation was mandatory.

We were instructed to go further north so that we could avoid any
potential danger. And of course, after experiencing Hurricane Katrina, not
too many people were willing to take any chances with Rita. Everybody was
trying to flee this storm, and they were moving fast to get out of harm's way.

USA Today reported that nearly 200 million people from the Louisiana
and Texas coasts tried to flee this hurricane, and the state of Texas was

trying hard to get more than 200,000 gallons of fuel to area gas stations in the Houston area. This storm was so serious that Rick Perry, the governor of Texas, said, "Be calm, be strong, say a prayer for Texas."

Our group of nearly 200 needed a plan for our second mass departure. So I needed to make some level-headed decisions fast. We quickly began to create another evacuation plan and prepared for the new journey ahead.

Again, a part of me was hoping that this storm would diminish and go away, because I did not want to have to move again. Initially, I thought perhaps we could build a church in Beaumont, Texas, which is about 11 miles outside of Lumberton, and maybe even build homes there, but something in my spirit had told me that we were not going to settle there. Actually, truth be told, I never had a real sense of peace in Lumberton. Not that the town was bad or anything, but I just didn't believe that God was calling us to establish ourselves there. And that was confirmed when we got word that Hurricane Rita was indeed headed our way. My wife still remembers how she felt when the news hit the airwaves:

Wife Claudette

> "When I heard that Rita was coming, I was like, 'Oh my goodness, another one!' At that moment, I immediately began praying that she would fade away. And if not, I was hoping that she wouldn't be as bad as the forecast, because the kids were finally getting settled into their new schools and meeting new friends. And having to move them again, let's just say that I wasn't looking forward to it. But on the contrary, if that is what God was saying, then who was I to object? At that point, I just needed to follow along with my husband and trust that the Lord would see us through yet another storm. He'd proven Himself faithful time and time again, so I thought surely He wouldn't forsake us now."

I got the idea that the Lord wanted us off the coastline. Our experience certainly seemed to be telling us the same thing. Now what that meant exactly, I didn't know. Nonetheless, I wasn't going to argue with Him. I believed that in time, it would be revealed. The Bible reminded me that His ways are not our ways, or His thoughts our thoughts (Isaiah 55:9). I simply needed to trust in the Lord that He was going to direct our path (Proverbs 3:5-6). By late Thursday night on September 22, as we were preparing to evacuate, Administrators Brian and Vicky at Church Alive's Retreat Center suggested that we go to another retreat center located in either Brownwood, Texas or Lakeview Baptist Assembly in Lone Star, Texas. I wasn't aware of any other places, so I asked them to check their availability and accommodations for our large group, and it turned out that both were available. So with that information, I made the decision to go to Brownwood, and informed our members that we would leave by midnight.

We quickly packed up as much as we could into our vehicles. It's amazing how much stuff you can accumulate in three weeks. There was such an abundance of supplies. The outpouring of God's love through the people in that community had been so great that we literally had to get a U-haul truck to transport our belongings. Even with the truck, we still had to leave some things behind to retrieve later because there was just no way that we were able to bring everything with us.

That evening, I hovered around the TV, watching the news carefully. I was really waiting to see if Hurricane Rita was going to change her path, but nothing changed. She was still headed for Texas and there was nothing we could do to stop her. I certainly wasn't going to try to weather this one out because I had too many people under my watch and care. I had to follow through with what I believed God was telling me to do, which was to pull our caravan out at midnight. Before leaving, though, we had to prepare for our journey ahead. Ralph Woods explains this process:

Ralph

"Before leaving, I took on the responsibility of making sure that all of the vehicles were gassed up, tires were checked and oil was changed. I made sure that every car had the proper liquids that it needed to withstand the journey. We didn't want to take any chances on cars breaking down in the midst of the evacuation because we didn't do our part. So a few of the brothers and myself came together to do our best to prevent break downs from happening. Then we all helped each other out by getting all the vehicles packed up and loaded for the trip. Every hand was needed. I just wanted to make sure that we were ready. And by 12:00 a.m., we were pulling out of the retreat center's parking lot."

* * *

As our forty-car caravan drove along, we saw cars, trucks, vans, mobile homes, U-hauls, you name it on the highways and back roads. People had tried to load up as much as they could into their vehicles. I mean, stuff was literally packed to the ceilings of cars, and even the hoods of SUVs were loaded with luggage, securely (we hoped) tied down. Man, we could empathize, because we knew from recent experience what it felt like to lose almost everything we owned.

While we drove, creeping inch by inch and bumper to bumper, I looked out of my window at the people in vehicles to the right and left of me. Some had countenances of fear, frustration, and uncertainty. Others, though, seemed to have a sense of peace. There were a lot of mixed emotions out there.

The best thing to do when you see someone who's having a difficult time dealing with a situation, whether you know them or not, is simply to pause and pray. The Bible says to "pray without ceasing" (1 Thessalonians 5:17) and to watch and pray (Luke 21:36). So as we traveled, I felt the need to simply pray for our ministry and for others along the way. God says in His Word, "If my people, which are called by My Name, shall humble themselves, and pray, and seek My face, and turn from their wicked ways; then will I hear from heaven, and will forgive their sin, and will heal their land" (2 Chronicles 7:14).

Prayer strengthens the spirit. And I knew that the Lord would give us the strength that we needed to endure whatever He decided to bring us through in this crisis.

* * *

While on the road, a few tests did pop up on us. Two of our members' cars broke down, and then another got into a car accident. So our whole caravan had to pull over for each of those incidents. We ended up having to abandon those vehicles (which we later retrieved). But we had to shift some families around to make it work, which it did. We were not leaving anyone behind. I didn't care what it took – if there was a will, there was a way. If there ever was a time for us to stick together, it was then.

But along the way, the Lord made the journey a little lighter for us. One of our members spotted a doughnut shop. I'm sure many of our stomachs were growling at the sight. So we all pulled over, ate doughnuts, and drank some hot chocolate and coffee. We all acted like it was a sort of mini-fellowship. It seemed as though we were being woven together, one event at a time. We were truly beginning to feel like we were one big family taking a very long road trip. The fact that the kids were having so much fun made the idea all the more real. Even our teenagers were getting along well, if you can imagine that. They were just laughing, talking, and kidding around.

When I looked at those little ones just giggling and horsing around, I felt like they already knew that everything was going to be okay. We can really learn from the little ones if we pay attention to them and to Scripture. Jesus said, "Verily I say unto you, Except ye be converted, and become as little children, ye shall not enter into the kingdom of heaven. Whosoever therefore shall humble himself as this little child, the same is greatest in the kingdom of heaven" (Matthew18:3-4).

So true! I knew without a shadow of a doubt that if we relaxed in God's presence and trusted Him along the way, that He would *eventually* (as my wife would often say) lead us to a safe place. All we needed to do at that time was to remain prayerful and faithful, and keep seeking Him. We would make it through.

* * *

As we continued to drive on the highway, we came across the scene of a really bad accident. Before we could reach the site of the crash, we saw a police officer standing in the middle of the road redirecting traffic. He flagged us down and told us that the road we were trying to travel on was closed – there was no entry. Now, we were not at all familiar with Texas' roads or highways. That was the only way we knew to get to Brownwood. So I took that as a sign that the Lord did not want us to go in that direction.

It really was like He sent an angel with a direct order to stop us in our tracks and reroute us to where He truly wanted us to go. So there we were again, having to trust God for a new direction. I remember asking Him, "Okay Lord, then if not there, where?" And then I received instant provision. Earlier, I, my wife, Brian and Vicky had looked into possibly going to another retreat center located in Lone Star, Texas at the Lakeview Baptist Assembly. I thanked God that we still had their information on us at the time. So we called and they told us that they still had room for our group.

I then turned back to the officer and asked him how to get to our alternative destination. Immediately, he pointed us in the right direction. I'll tell you, we'd had our plans all worked out. But God had another one in store for us. His Word says, "We can make our plans, but the Lord determines our steps" (Proverbs 16:9 NLT).

After we'd received the new directions, I let everyone know that we were headed to an alternate location. So our entire caravan turned around and started driving towards Lone Star. Consequently, a trip that would have typically taken us four hours took us *nineteen* hours because of rerouting and traffic. Add to that the summer heat; hours in a cramped car full of people, pillows, blankets, snacks, and luggage; and bumper to bumper traffic with your windows rolled down to preserve gas (keep in mind that there were millions of Texans and New Orleanians who were on the road all at once, and that gas was very limited at every station). It was pretty rough. Erika Chapman recalls her experience:

Erika

"While we were on road, I remember how hot it was and how slow the traffic was moving. Just to give someone an idea of how slow the flow of traffic was, several of us from our church got out of our vehicles to use the restroom at a nearby vacant church on the side of the road. But when we headed back, we noticed that the cars had barely moved but maybe a couple of feet, if that. We were so amazed that we were traveling at such a reduced speed. I had never experienced anything like that before in my life. Thank God the caravan didn't leave us. Just kidding! I know our pastor wouldn't have left us stranded out there. But it was truly a mind-blowing and unforgettable experience."

Compared to when we evacuated from New Orleans, this trip was almost harder because we hadn't mapped out a route to our next location in advance. It felt like we were in uncharted waters. Plus, the journey seemed longer and perhaps more convoluted just because of the incredible number of people out on the road. Not only were there evacuees from New Orleans on the road, but also people from Houston and other surrounding towns who were trying to flee this storm. Dedrick Thompson remembers the trip all too well:

Dedrick

"It was an extremely long drive. I couldn't get comfortable, we were actually living out of suitcases like homeless people, and my 1988 Ford Taurus was stuffed to capacity. I wasn't even sure if it would make it. The drive was really beginning to take its toll on me, because I was ready to get settled. A couple of times, I contemplated leaving the church group to go stay somewhere and really get settled. I was like, 'Man, I got my four month old son and my wife out here. We could go stay with some family members until the church finds a place.' I wanted to throw in the towel. I was weary and trying to fight off sleep. I was like, 'Lord, I'm disgusted. I'm tired, I can't go anymore, I'm tired of driving, and my wife is going to sleep on me.' And then, while I was creeping along at about five miles per hour, I actually fell asleep behind the wheel. Brother Calvin came running up to my car to wake me up – turns out, I was holding up the line. The Lord really used him, because I was exhausted. Every now and then, he would pop back up and check on me to make sure that I was awake. One time he even brought me a cold soft drink to help keep me going. In the midst of it all, I have to say that God kept me. Even in my aggravation, He was patient with me. I knew enough to reflect on His faithfulness. During that ride, I was able to look back and remember all that He'd done for me and my family in the previous year, and how He'd blessed us through our recent wedding and in ministry. I was in full-time ministry and loving it, until Hurricanes Katrina and Rita came rushing in. It was like God was showing me the mountain top experience and the valley low. It's like being on cloud nine one moment in life and then playing handball on the curb the next (as my pastor would say). That's when the Lord began to speak to me, saying, 'I know you're upset with me in 2005, but look back at what I did for you in 2004.' Right then, I knew that I needed to praise Him, trust Him in spite of my circumstances, and rely on His faithfulness."

Even though the trip was long, we didn't get discouraged or give up. We just kept going, even when a few of our members decided to veer off on their own to figure out a faster way to get to the retreat center…and got lost. Now, it took a couple of extra hours for us to find them. Truth be told, that was frustrating. We used our cell phones to guide members back to our route, and eventually everybody found their way back on the road together. I guess God figured we needed a few bumps in the road to show us that we need Him *every* step of the way.

* * *

While we drove, some marriages were even been stitched back together. Donita Richard testifies to God's hidden plan to save her marriage of nine years during a nineteen hour drive to the retreat center:

Donita

"When we initially evacuated for the first storm, Hurricane Katrina, my husband and I had been separated for a year. Though we attended the same church, we were no longer together. I was living in the House of Leah with our three children and he was staying at the House of Joseph. I was a woman scorned from the pain of my husband committing adultery on me. I was eagerly searching for emotional healing from the Lord, and I knew that if there ever was a chance of us getting back together again, my husband would have to get his life on track spiritually, because without a personal relationship with Jesus Christ and a born-again lifestyle, I was not going to consider reconciliation. When the time came to evacuate, I still had possession of our one car. For the kids' sake, it was recommended that we ride together to get out of harm's way. That was definitely a set up by God, because I would have never done that on my own. During the drive to Lumberton, we actually had a chance to really talk about some things. It was as if God was connecting the links that were missing in our relationship. When we had to leave again for Hurricane Rita, this time, we didn't dread the ride. We figured God was allowing us more time to work things out. I believe the Lord was mending and healing my broken heart with every mile. I needed to be able to forgive him for hurting me, and he realized that he needed to be more patient, understanding, responsible, and diligent in the things of God. The Lord was truly working from the inside out. I know without a shadow of a doubt that God used the storms to help restore my marriage. We actually were able to become friends, which was incredible because even before our separation, we weren't really friends. So the long drives helped bring us closer together, not only as husband and wife, but as a family again. If those storms had not come in our lives when they did, I don't know if we would've ever gotten back together."

This was indeed, a divine intervention. Psalm 147:3 (NIV) says, "He heals the broken hearted and binds up their wounds." Through the hurricanes, these two were healed. Their story is one of godly reunion and reconciliation. God knew before they were formed in their mothers' wombs that this day would come. It just took the storms to bring it forth.

* * *

Finally, we reached our destination: the Lakeview Baptist Assembly Retreat Center. The staff there greeted us from the road and directed our large caravan to the parking area, and from the first moments, they welcomed us with open arms – probably not an easy task, considering we were hot, hungry, and exhausted when we stepped out of those vehicles, and probably didn't smell very good either.

We were absolutely relieved when we learned that the staff had prepared a hot buffet-style meal for us. I mean, we had everything from tacos to burgers, baked and fried chicken, fries, macaroni and cheese, beans, mashed potatoes, hot buttered rolls, and so much more. Plus, there was an assortment of desserts and soft drinks. God really showed up and showed out on that one! He expressed His great love once again for us through those kind and generous people. I think I can speak on behalf of our entire ministry when I say that we were very grateful for their warm Texas welcome and for God's redirection.

Speaking of redirection, I have to give thanks to God for rerouting us to Lone Star instead of Brownwood, because, knowing what I know now, it would have been much harder to make it there. The drive would have been even longer, and I believe that many of our members might have passed out on the side of the road or in their cars from heat exhaustion. Plus, we had elderly folks with us who needed to eat, take meds, and get some rest from the road. It would have been taxing on all of us to drive further. But God knew, in His perfect timing, when and where we were to take a break from the road and find the right place to rest.

After we had eaten our fill, we made up new sleeping arrangements. At this retreat center, there were plenty of dorm rooms available. There were also a few cabins, so we issued those to individuals with special needs and to a few of our ministers. I didn't hear any complaints, because, for the most part, everyone realized the extraordinary nature of our journey, and we were seeing the hand of God making a way for us. We were just so thankful that we had a place to lay our heads to rest.

*　*　*

While we were there, the staff provided three full meals for us every day! There was a buffet-style breakfast every morning with grits, scrambled eggs, pancakes, biscuits, bacon, sausage, fruit, and juice. For lunch, there were hamburgers, nuggets, and fries for the kids as well as hotdogs and sandwiches for the adults, and dinner was always a wonderful buffet.

To help pass the time, most of us enjoyed the countryside and the center itself. Some members went fishing, like my wife's mother who traveled with us, Ella Louise Ford (better known as "Momie" to the church). Here is what she said:

Momie

"It wasn't a stressful time for me at all. To be honest, I really enjoyed myself. I enjoyed fishing, the food was great, and I had fun hanging out with my new fishing buddies: Tiffany Thomas, Johnny Williams, Derrick Washington, and Ernest Schuster. We fished all day and night. I remember we would run back and forth to the local fish and tackle shop near the center to get our bait and fishing supplies. And we would talk and share a few laughs together along the way. Oh, I had a grand time. Sometimes the little kids would come running down there to the dock and disturb the fish. But that only made my time there more memorable. I would say, though, the best part about the whole ordeal was that I made new friends."

Yeah, I would agree that she really enjoyed the fishing. And that was good. God knew exactly what everybody needed to help see us through. There were others who played tether ball and football, read books, and talked in small group settings, while some went hiking on nature trails or just sat by the lake to pray or meditate on the Word of God.

*   *   *

At night, the dorm rooms and cabins were filled to capacity. The teenage boys could be found huddled up playing video games, while the men would sit around talking. My wife said the women were simply taking care of their children and getting to know one another better. Tiffany Thomas describes what she encountered in her dorm room:

Tiffany

"There were eight sets of bunk beds in the room where I was assigned, and there were about ten of us in the room. I was a single woman and I shared the room with a few other single women. But a few married ladies were with us too, and some of them were mothers who had their toddlers and school-aged daughters with them. We had a good mix. Honestly, once we got settled, we had fun. And it wasn't long before the room began to look like a typical ladies' dorm room. There were curling irons all over the bathroom countertops, with blow dryers, hair brushes and combs, jewelry, and make-up, not to mention the many damp towels hung to dry from the morning showers. We would stay up late at night talking, sharing testimonies, and watching movies, while really getting a chance to get to know each other. Prior to the storms, we would see each other in church week after week, but, to be candid, we really didn't know one another. I believe this was God's way of bringing us

together as a body of believers in a very unique way to get
us to understand the true importance of unity and being a
church family. And we had fun doing it."

I believe that it was a time of unity, and that God was birthing something
new in us as a ministry. Of course, anytime God begins to birth a new thing,
it's not always a flower bed of ease. Sometimes when change begins to take
shape, there can be a little bit of friction. And we experienced that firsthand
when a few arguments broke forth.

We had a lot of different personalities coming together in one place, and
for that long of a period of time, and in a crisis situation. For some, tension
was beginning to rise. Although the issues were rectified immediately, I
couldn't stress enough that we all needed to stay in constant prayer and in
the Word of God. I tried my best to help everyone understand how not to
allow the storms to get their spirits down. This was not the time to be acting
out of character with one another. And I was serious about not bickering,
murmuring, and complaining. It had to be nipped in the bud. The Israelites
had to walk around for forty years in the desert because of their complaining
tongues, and I was trying to keep us from wandering all over the state of
Texas longer than necessary.

So no matter the upheaval going on around us, I continued to have
normally scheduled church services, such as our Bible studies and prayer
meetings. I knew that we needed to stay grounded in the Word of God
to help keep us strong. Trials come to test our faith and can sometimes
bring out stuff in us that people wouldn't imagine. But Jesus reminds us in
John 16:33 (NLT), "I have told you all this so that you may have peace in
Me. Here on earth you will have many trials and sorrows. But take heart,
because I have overcome the world." And I believe that the Lord will help us
to overcome anything when we trust Him. My daughter Demaries Glaspie
can attest to this:

Demaries

"Initially, I tell you no lie, it was not easy for me to trust
God on this one. Already, I didn't like long drives, and

driving in a convoy was even worse. Then I was staying in dorms away from my husband. Don't get me wrong, I was thankful that the Lord provided a way of escape for us and a roof over our heads, but it was still hard for me. I cried, I clashed with a few people, and while we were in Lakeview, I actually considered breaking camp. I even tried to convince my husband that we could go stay with some old friends of mine who'd invited us to come to their house in Lyndel, Texas until the church got settled. I could sense that he wasn't in agreement with me, and when we talked it over with my mom and dad, they told us, 'You can go if you want to, but it's almost as if you're running out on us because it's hard. And we could use your help around here to labor with others.' Even though they had a good point, I still felt inconvenienced and upset. I knew that I needed to consider my husband who was in fact a minister in training at the time, our children, and others around me, but it was tough. I felt that I just needed to get away to breathe, to think, to cry. And when I got to my dorm room, no one was there. God had allotted me that time to be alone. I remember lying on the bed, crying, while I popped in a new CD by Marvin Sapp entitled *Be Exalted*. On the album, one of the songs that I hit unintentionally was called 'Trust in You.' The song kept playing over and over again, singing, 'You've been so faithful…Lord, I put my trust in You.' All of a sudden, my flesh was dying on the inside and my will was breaking. Then I began saying to God through the tears, 'Yes Lord, I'm going to trust You. I just need You to strengthen me right now. I need You to carry me through this. I don't want to be out of *Your* will. Help me Lord to trust and obey Your plan.' I believe that was my breakthrough moment. Somehow I knew that Jesus was going to work it all out for not only my good, but for the good of all of us as a church. I just needed to trust Him."

The Bible says in Psalm 34:18 (NLT) "The Lord is close to the brokenhearted; He rescues those whose spirits are crushed." Demaries was set free that evening. We needed her. She was an intricate piece not only of our family, but our church. I'm pretty sure at some point, a few others may have been having those same feelings and wondering what God was doing through all of this. Yet, all we needed to do was trust that the Lord knew the plans that He had for us.

When I look back on it today, I strongly believe that the Lord was doing a *shaking* through the storms. At that time within our ministry, we experienced incredible surges of deliverance. Many were being purged and purified in the spirit. And when I consider the fact that the name Katrina means "pure," it all makes perfect sense. God was testing our hearts to see if we would trust Him in spite of our circumstances. He wanted us to get to know Him more while leaving our old comforts and pasts behind...no turning back.

*   *   *

After Hurricane Rita had passed and Houston's residents had gone back to their homes, we received word that Lumberton had been hit pretty badly and that the retreat center where we'd first evacuated to had suffered some major damages and needed to be rebuilt. We also discovered that some of the belongings that we'd left behind had been destroyed. The owners of the retreat center hired a construction company to not only work on the facility, but to also reside there until they'd completed the work. They welcomed us to return but mentioned that we would have to share the dormitory with the men there. Well, I knew that wasn't going to work, because I had men, women, teenagers, and children that I was responsible for, and I just couldn't take the risk of foul play. So I began to seek God again for provision.

After staying at the Lakeview Baptist Retreat Center in Lone Star for about two weeks, I got word that the owners had pre-booked another group for a conference prior to our arrival. At that point, I was like, "Okay, God; now what?" But not all was lost – the staff soon told us that we did not have to leave and that we could occupy another center on the other side of their property. At first, I thought that could work. But when my wife and I surveyed the land, we quickly realized that it was *much* smaller than what we already had. So even though we appreciated the offer and the new accommodations, we both knew that it was not going to work with a group of our size.

Again, I found myself seeking the Lord in prayer, asking, "Lord, what do you want me to do with all of your people? Where do you want us to go from here?" I didn't know what God was doing. But I knew enough to wait for an answer. Finally, within a day, His direction came. He quickened me to inform all of our members that it was time to pack up everything again because we were hitting the road. This time we were headed for Dallas, Texas – the "Big D!"

After Hurricane Katrina's destructive impact, millions of New Orleanians and Houstonians flee Hurricane Rita's coming fury. Due to the high traffic volume, it took us nineteen hours to reach Lakeview Baptist Assembly in Lone Star, Texas.

CHAPTER FIVE:

Pathway to Purpose

Dallas, Texas

"Trust in the Lord with all thine heart; and lean not unto thine own understanding. In all thy ways acknowledge Him, and He shall direct thy paths. Be not wise in thine own eyes: fear the Lord, and depart from evil."

Proverbs 3:5-7

By this time, Hurricane Rita had passed and most travelers were either headed east to go back home to the Houston area or they were biding their time in area hotels until the damage was cleared out of their towns. Meanwhile, approximately 200 of us were still riding together in a caravan, traveling on the highway headed toward our *third* destination.

Dallas was our next stop. We had thought of Dallas because many hotels were still booked solid going south, east, and west because of both hurricanes. All we could do was go north. And the Holiday Inn Select Hotel by the Dallas Airport was the only available hotel that could house all of us. So we made the reservation.

The trip was smooth and steady and clearly orchestrated by the Lord. Not that the other trips weren't coordinated by Him, but during this particular one, we didn't experience any extended hours of traffic.

When we arrived at the hotel, the staff welcomed us with friendly customer service and a comfortable atmosphere. God had provided once again for His people! The Lord had covered us financially by using FEMA to help pay for our rooms once again. Here, families were able to sleep together again and singles were able to get a bit of privacy. These new accommodations were a relief for our married couples who had been split up thus far. It was great to see them all together again!

Once more, the Lord had supplied us with food, shelter, and rest. Jesus said in Matthew 11:28 (NIV), "Come to me, all you who are weary and burdened, and I will give you rest." The room that my wife and I shared was pretty comfortable and relaxing. We enjoyed it. I remember that during our stay, many of us looked forward to the breakfast that the hotel made available every morning. I'd never seen a hotel breakfast quite like it – I mean, this one in particular was in abundance! Every morning there was this full breakfast buffet-style assortment of cereal, juices, yogurt, fruit, grits, waffles, and scrambled eggs, not to mention the loaded omelets served to your taste. God was so good to us! I enjoyed every bite.

* * *

Well, I can honestly say that Dallas lived up to its name, the "Big D." It is a very big city! It has a lot of highways, byways, crossroads, service roads, big buildings, and countless surrounding counties. Plus, it's fast and busy. Although we came from a pretty well known and highly populated city, Dallas was another world for us. Not only that, but considering all that we were already dealing with at the time, it seemed too big and very overwhelming.

Traveling from county to county was beginning to take its toll on some of us. I remember feeling like we were pilgrims voyaging in a strange land. Truth be told, we were still homeless. I would say about 85% of our members, including my wife and I, had no home to go back to. If someone would have told me this beforehand, I would have created a *How to Prevent Yourself from Being Homeless after a Storm* plan, and it would have been one of the agenda items for our annual leadership meeting that year. I'm just jiving! But it just goes to show you how we never really know what God will do to get us to fulfill His purposes in our lives.

Anyhow, for the most part, we were thankful and were having a pleasant stay. However, I knew that God was not calling us to settle down in Dallas.

It wasn't reconciled in my spirit that this was where He wanted us to reside. And if I would have taken it on without God's direction, I would have made a huge mess of things – not only for me, but for my entire congregation. I couldn't take that kind of a risk. I was still on the pathway to God's purpose for my ministry. So at that moment in time, I just needed to hold steady and continue to pray and to seek God for direction. I kept following His ways, because I knew that He knew what was best for us in the end.

*   *   *

In the meantime, we were able to utilize the hotel's main conference room to hold our church services, which was a great blessing. We never stopped having church! We had our Bible studies and Sunday service in the conference room, and held our corporate prayer time in one of the local parks. We needed it all in order to keep us strong in the Lord. We had to stay connected to the Father. He was going to help us survive the outcome of these storms together.

The Word of the Lord was still going forth, and lives were being changed and renewed. I had always wanted to be an evangelist, though God had seen fit to make me a pastor, and this was the closest I ever came to being a traveling minister.

As the days passed, I realized that just like there's power in prayer, there's strength in numbers. We needed to encourage and help each other along the way. The Bible speaks of this: "Let us think of ways to motivate one another to acts of love and good works. And let us not neglect our meeting together, as some people do, but encourage one other, especially now that the day of His return is drawing near" (Hebrews 10:24-25 NLT). Truth be told, we thrived on acts of love and encouragement. Viola Chapman shares on the importance of love:

Viola

"On Sunday, October 2nd, our pastor taught on love. I can honestly say that one of the things that really helped keep us together as a church was *love*. No matter what anyone needed, someone was always right there to help. If you needed a shoulder to cry on, someone was there to help wipe the tears. When you needed someone to talk to, someone was there to listen. When I was happy and dancing for the Lord, someone was right there to dance with me. We were literally all in the same shoes. We were all equal. No one had more than the other. We were all thrust into one direction all at once. We comforted one another through every step. And even though some of us had our differences of opinion on some things and had short fuses at times, we still managed to stick together and keep the peace because we didn't know what tomorrow held. More importantly, we needed to practice what we'd been taught in church and through the Scriptures on *how* we needed to love one another in spite of our differences and circumstances. So I would say that it was God's gracious spirit of love that rained over us, and kept us together as a church."

I would agree that love plays a vital role in any given situation in our lives. God shows us His love through others, and, most importantly, through the blood sacrifice of His Son Jesus Christ. Jesus told us that loving God *is* the greatest commandment (Matthew 22:37-39) and we should love our neighbors as ourselves. We are also reminded that "Love is patient and kind. Love is not jealous or boastful or proud or rude. It does not demand its own way. It is not irritable, and it keeps no record of being wronged. It does not rejoice about injustice but rejoices whenever the truth wins out. Love never gives up, never loses faith, is always hopeful, and endures through every circumstance" (1 Corinthians 13:4-7 NLT). God is love. And we're worthy of receiving it.

* * *

The Lord was moving mightily in the midst of our travels. Every now and then, a few visitors would come in to worship with us and some even accepted Jesus Christ as their Lord and Savior. I specifically recall a young man who had evacuated from Lumberton with us rededicating his life to the Lord and being delivered from a life of drugs and the roughness of the city streets. The Bible says in 1 John 1:9, "If we confess our sins, He is faithful and just to forgive us our sins, and to cleanse us from all unrighteousness." That was awesome! The angels rejoiced, and so did we!

One evening after I'd preached, something hit me like a ton of bricks: *I seriously did not know what God was doing or where we were going next.* I had come to a place of *great* uncertainty. I did not understand what was happening and I couldn't see clearly. At that point, I began to ask, "Lord, what is happening here? Where are You?" Granted, I knew He was there, but I believe He was testing me to see if I would continue to follow His plan, even when I couldn't see the way.

Then a Scripture came to mind: "Trust in the Lord with all thine heart; and lean not unto thine own understanding. In all thy ways acknowledge Him, and He shall direct thy paths. Be not wise in thine own eyes: fear the Lord..." (Proverbs 3:5-7). This verse helped keep me balanced as I tried to avoid the trap of figuring things out on my own. It kept me believing in the fact that God was still in control over the situation, and that I could definitely trust in Him – not my feelings.

So I stayed on my face in prayer for my wife, the church members, and for my own strength as the pastor and shepherd of my flock. I had to remain very sensitive for the sound of the Lord's voice while waiting for *His* instruction. I did not know where we were going next, and it seemed like *God was silent*. In the past, I have experienced His silence. Sometimes when God is quiet, it means that we're either in error and need to repent, or we just need to continue waiting on His perfect timing. I knew that I was at a moment of waiting.

I resolved to just sit back and wait patiently for Him to respond. I knew that I needed to rest in Him and not be anxious for an answer. The Bible says, "Do not be anxious about anything, but in everything by prayer and supplication with thanksgiving let your requests be made known to God" (Philippians 4:6 ESV). I admit, it wasn't very easy, but it was very necessary.

We were still waiting for news from city officials in New Orleans on whether or not we would be able to go back home anytime soon. However, due to the breach in the levees and the damage that the water had done to buildings, houses included, we were not allowed to move back into the city just yet. It wasn't safe or sanitary due to downed power lines and sewage issues.

So Lumberton was no longer an option, Lakeview Baptist Assembly was booked, Dallas was too big, and New Orleans wasn't ready. We didn't really know what we were going to do!

*   *   *

It was now the beginning of October, and, after staying at the hotel for almost a week, one morning I awoke to a sudden change in the atmosphere. The weather in Dallas had turned cold, and all of us were still in summer clothes. I'll never forget that time because our children did not have any sweaters, coats, hats, or boots. We hadn't planned to be away from home long enough for the weather to change! Although we were in an uncomfortable spot, I was reminded of God's Word: "Therefore I tell you, do not worry about your life, what you will eat or drink; or about your body, what you will wear. Is not life more important than food, and the body more important than clothes? Look at the birds of the air; they do not sow or reap or store away in barns, and yet your heavenly Father feeds them. Are you not much more valuable than they?" (Matthew 6:25-26 NIV). God shows us through this Scripture that we are worth more to Him than birds, so we need not worry. He promises to continue to provide for us, and in our present situation, He certainly did. Through financial support from FEMA and the Red Cross, we were able to get everything that we needed!

I honestly believe that even in this fairly favorable situation, God was testing us to see how we would respond. I remember reading again about the Israelites and how they complained profusely in the wilderness and upset God when things changed. As a result, they missed out on the very blessings and promises that He had in store for them. Simply put, the Lord hates complaining. In Philippians 2:14, the Scriptures tell us: "Do all things without murmurings and disputings."

In his day, Moses told the Israelites, "When the Lord heard your complaining, He became very angry. So He solemnly swore, 'Not one of you from this wicked generation will live to see the good land I swore to give your ancestors'" (Deuteronomy 1:34-35 NLT). David Armour gives his take on the experience:

David

"I was definitely comparing this time to the days of Moses and the Israelites. I was actually fixated on the similarity! God had provided for all of our needs, was bringing us through foreign lands as His people, and He was not only feeding us natural food, but spiritual food as well through our pastor. This was fascinating to me! From my perspective, I believe that the Lord was keeping us and showing us His awesome favor and love through all sorts of people and ways, because our pastor loved Him and was faithful to His Word and followed His commands. Our pastor never gave up. He kept praying, preaching, teaching, counseling, and leading us, all the while remaining strong supernaturally through God. And as a result, God was faithful to us. Deuteronomy 7:9 (NLT) says, 'Understand, therefore, that the Lord your God is indeed God. He is the faithful God who keeps His covenant for a thousand generations and lavishes His unfailing love on those who love Him and obey His commands.' I also believe that the Lord was testing all of us as a ministry for something greater. He had something awesome in store for us! We just didn't know what it was at the time. But whatever it was, I didn't want to forfeit it by acting out of character in the wilderness like the Israelites did. So I was very prayerful. All I knew was that we just needed to be ready and open for whatever God was going to bring us through to receive the promises that awaited us. And in that case, murmuring and complaining was not an option."

Well, I must agree. I was not trying to recreate ancient Biblical history with my church, and I certainly didn't want to miss out on the promises of God due to complaints. So we remained prayerful that we would not grumble about whatever state God had us in at the time. And I was also praying that my congregation would just be thankful and content in the process. Paul said in Philippians 4:11, "Not that I speak in respect of want: for I have learned, in whatsoever state I am, therewith to be content." The Bible also says, "But godliness with contentment is great gain" (1 Timothy 6:6). So we needed to watch our character very closely while we waited for the promises of God.

*　*　*

On Thursday, October 6, change found us once again. The hotel manager called me and informed me that we were going to have to relocate because there was a big college football game between the Texas Longhorns and the Oklahoma Sooners that weekend and the hotel was booked solid for football players and other guests. My answer had arrived! God was saying that it was time to *Mount Up* again. I didn't know where, but I was not leaning on my own understanding, just trusting in the Lord.

As in the Old Testament days, the "cloud" of His Spirit was moving. Exodus 13:21 (NLT) reads, "The Lord went ahead of them. He guided them during the day with a pillar of cloud, and He provided light at night with a pillar of fire. This allowed them to travel by day or by night." So as people of God, we were in essence following the cloud! We were following the Lord as He was leading and guiding us with His Presence and His Holy Spirit. I had to depend upon the fact that *He* knew the pathway to our purpose.

With that in mind, we moved on to our *fourth* destination, which was none other than the capital of Texas!

We took a picture of the Holiday Inn Select sign as a remembrance of our stop there. This is me preaching in Dallas and some of us loading up our bags in the U-Haul truck. We were preparing to hit the road again. This is also when Dallas had turned cold.

CHAPTER SIX:

Anchored in the Lord

Austin and Burnet, Texas

"But they that wait upon the Lord shall renew their strength;
they shall mount up with wings as eagles; they shall run,
and not be weary; and they shall walk, and not faint."
Isaiah 40:31

On the afternoon of October 7, 2005, we arrived in the northern part of Austin, Texas. Our destination was the AmeriSuites Hotel. Some of our members drove ahead of us with maps and directions, and that was fine. However, my wife and I and a few other members who followed us got lost. Granted, we were within minutes of the place the whole time, and we had directions as well, but the way Interstate 183 is designed confused us more than a little bit.

We could see the hotel from the interstate, but we kept driving by and passing it up. Then we'd get off at one exit only to find that we had missed it. We'd get back on the interstate only to discover that we'd missed it again. So we just kept going around and around and around. It was quite frustrating. Fortunately, Anthony Torns, one of our members, peeked out from the window of his hotel suite and happened to see us just going around in circles. He called my wife on her cell phone and told her that he could see us looping around, and he explained to us how to put a halt to what seemed like a merry-go-round ride gone completely wrong.

I breathed a sigh of relief when we finally got off the highway and were able to check in to the hotel. However, after I'd walked into our suite, dropped my bags, and sat down to get settled, the Lord instantly revealed that we were only to stay at that hotel for *one* day. Immediately, my wife and I began to search for a new location. Shortly thereafter, we received word from a local contact that there was a lodge in Burnet that had enough space available to accommodate our large group. On that note, I started making provisions to get back on the road the very next day to head toward a place called the Canyon of the Eagles Lodge and Nature Park.

* * *

On Saturday, October 8, 2005, I awakened to a new day. The temperature in the room was cool and the halls were quiet. I remember pulling back the curtains to see the sun breaking through the dark morning clouds. I'm an early riser, so it was normal for me to get up before everyone else. On a typical morning back in New Orleans, I would get up right before dawn to study and inquire of the Lord His direction, wisdom, knowledge, and revelation. But on that particular day, it was different. I wasn't sitting at my desk hungrily thumbing through the Scriptures; instead, I found myself positioned quietly before the Lord near the windowsill of a hotel suite far away from home, praying for strength and wisdom to lead my congregation and family to a safe place.

My members had no idea the amount of stress that was upon me at that time. I guess I looked like I was fine. But how could they know? I was their pastor. I may have appeared strong before them, but I was weak and humble before the Lord. Back in 1976, the Lord saved me, and for the next twenty years, He prepared me for Smoking for Jesus Ministry. I had to be humble before God – He had blessed me with all that I had, including the responsibility to seek His direction for His flock.

I resolved a long time ago to lay down my life and feelings for the sake of others. Surely I couldn't back up or back out in troubled times. The thought *never* crossed my mind to leave my members in the wilderness wandering around to fend for their own lives. I had a responsibility to God to look after those who had been entrusted to me. I wasn't an evangelist – I was a pastor. I labored, taught, counseled, and prayed with people week after week in the time leading up to the storm. I simply couldn't abandon ship just because the waters had gotten rough. I needed to stay anchored in the Lord and look toward the hills from which my help came from for strength (Psalm 121:1-2). The Lord was my peace in the midst of the storm, my strong tower, my lighthouse. Daily, I sought Him…*for all of us.*

* * *

Once again, it was time to move further along in our journey. I'd already informed everyone the night before to prepare for the trip ahead. I mentioned that if anyone needed to use the restrooms, get snacks for the road, etc., to please do so before getting on the highway. We wanted to make as few stops as possible. So bright and early the next morning, everyone loaded up their cars and got ready to go! Upon our checkout, we thanked the hotel staff for making our stay there very welcoming and for all of their help in such a short period of time. Around 6:00 a.m., we pulled our caravan out of the hotel parking lot and headed toward our next destination.

As we started driving north of Austin toward the town of Burnet, I learned that we were headed into an area called the Hill Country. Now in my mind, I was thinking, "Hmm, the hill country…That sounds familiar." I soon realized I was thinking of the Old Testament period when God told Moses, "It is time to break camp and move on. Go to the hill country…" (Deuteronomy 1:7 NLT).

For a second, I thought to myself, "What is God really doing? We're from the city. And we're headed to the hill country?" I wasn't complaining, though, because above all else, I banked on the fact that the Lord knew what He was doing. He had a plan for us – even if *I* didn't know what it was at the time. So I hearkened to His voice, obeyed His direction, and we proceeded to the hill country.

* * *

It's important to note that by this point, we'd already traveled to four different locations within the state of Texas…and we were on our way to the *fifth*. I honestly didn't know when it would end. Although I was getting

71

a little weary moving from city to city, I looked to this Scripture to keep me grounded: "And let us not be weary in well doing: for in due season we shall reap, if we faint not" (Galatians 6:9). I'm telling you, the Bible aided me tremendously during this process. I also had to rely heavily on the Word that was already within me over years of study, memorizing and meditating of Scriptures.

As we drove to the Canyon of the Eagles, which is about an hour and a half northwest of Austin, we couldn't help but find ourselves in awe of the countryside. Courtnaye Richard recalls her observations of the roadside view:

Courtnaye

> "On our way to the Canyon of the Eagles, the scenery was absolutely breathtaking. As we drove along the curvy and steep countryside of Highway 2341, I was blessed to see God's magnificent creation up close and personal. Being a city girl, the view was irresistible – overlooking the grassy hills and valleys, rich green trees, sparkling lakes and streams, and multi-colored flowers. And there was such an abundance of wildlife, beautiful butterflies, and birds, especially the eagles we saw periodically soaring high through the early morning sky. It was simply refreshing! Almost like a slice of heaven. For me, it was an unforgettable moment that will remain etched in my mind and heart forever."

We had never seen anything quite like it. It was as if God had carved out this place just for us to experience His greatness. We were blown away that the Lord would be gracious enough to allow us to encounter His hand at work in the earth in such a beautiful way.

Around 8:00 a.m. that Saturday morning, we pulled into the Canyon of the Eagles' parking lot. The Canyon of the Eagles is located just east of Lake Buchanan and the city of Buchanan Dam, north of Marble Falls. Even though this drive had been shorter and more enjoyable than our other trips, we were still very relieved to get out of our cars and leave them behind for a few days. The kids ran to find their friends while the teenagers popped on their mp3 players and began to look around, and some adults also took a quick walk around the new place. As for me and my wife, we walked over to the registration desk to get us all checked-in.

We quickly discovered that our check-in time wasn't until 3:00 p.m. Until then, the owner allowed us to wait in the main conference room. We waited patiently, talking, reading, and playing games for the next few hours. After a while, one of the staff members walked in and informed us that our cabins were ready. And everyone was off!

Expectantly, men, women, and teenagers hurriedly walked to their cabins to relax a bit and wash up, while the children ran around cheerfully, playing with friends (under supervision, of course). After my wife and I had gotten settled in, we walked around to check out the lodge and to see how we could arrange our church services and figure out meal schedules. We also wanted to look into a few excursions for our group to help pass the time, at least until God gave me direction for the next stop. So we met with the retreat director and the staff to see how their facility might be able to assist us, and they were very friendly and accommodating.

*　*　*

After they showed us around, we quickly realized that God had blessed us once again with His unmerited favor! All of our meals were provided, the cabins were covered through FEMA, and the facility was big enough to house all of our prayer meetings, Bible studies, and church services. And to help pass the time, there was a recreational room that contained a huge selection of board games; a table on which you could play checkers, dominoes, and pool; a big screen television; and a seating area great for lounging or holding group discussions. Most of the teenagers, and a few adults, really enjoyed that room.

It was a very serene and peaceful place, and it was also very well-known to neighboring residents and visitors for its special features and amenities such as the pier; fishing docks; hiking trails; nature walks; camping grounds; river-related activities like kayaking, sailing, and paddle-boating; and the recreational center. In addition, some people in the area highly recommended the nearby riverboat trip called the Vanishing Texas River Cruise. I didn't know if we were going to get a chance to explore or experience everything, but while we were there, I left it open to everyone to take advantage of what was available to us.

Some men went nature hiking, while a few married couples went off along the walking trails to talk. A lot of the women hung out in the courtyard fellowshipping. And of course, some people, like Anthony Torns, went fishing. He recalls his time on the river dock:

Anthony

"I love fishing, so I was glad that this place had somewhere I could fish. Just about every morning, I would gather a few of the brothers from the church and we'd head to the dock and cast a line until the late evening. We would joke, talk, and kick the Word around. It was cool, because it gave us a sense of peace in the midst of everything that was going on around us. I remember also that just about every morning before I met up with the guys, I would take a brief moment to pray. And I would not only intercede for my family, friends, and fellow church members, but I covered my pastor and his wife in prayer also. That was important, because I could only imagine the pressure that they were under throughout this whole ordeal. I knew that my pastor needed to hear clearly from the Lord for direction to lead us every day. We were all trusting that the Lord would use him to speak to us to reveal His plan through this journey. So prayer was essential. The Bible tells us to intercede for our leaders and those who are in authority over us. 1 Timothy 2:2 (NLT) says, 'Pray this way for kings and all who are in authority so that we can live peaceful and quiet lives marked by godliness and dignity.' Our pastor also taught us that sometimes you have to forget about what you're going through and how you feel to consider and pray for someone else. In doing so, the Lord will take care of you. I can honestly say that the Word of the Lord combined with divine wisdom from our pastor was true, because God did provide for us...every step of the way."

There is power in prayer. And I'm thankful that Anthony prayed for us. I coveted all of our members' prayers, because we needed it.

*   *   *

After being at the Canyon of the Eagles for a couple of days, my wife and I took a day to drive into Pflugerville, Hutto, Austin, Buda, and the surrounding areas to look for housing for all of us. I believed that God was in the midst of our search. I sought Him regarding this, because I certainly didn't want to be spinning my wheels looking for places only to later discover that it was me trying to make something happen. After being in ministry for almost 30 years, surely I knew better than that. But I also knew that faith without works is dead (James 2:17). And I'd sensed strongly that the Lord was indeed ordering my steps (Psalm 37:23).

While we were gone, many of our members decided to go on the river boat cruise. Calvin J. Richard, Jr. recalls his experience on the cruise and the area we were living in at the time:

Calvin

"Basically it was like we were having one BIG camping trip with our whole family. We were city folk, so to see deer, skunks, eagles, rattle snakes, huge road lizards, big mosquitoes, bats, possums, and a family of raccoons fighting for our leftovers – it was straight crazy! And there were bald eagles flying around freely. We had to watch our little kids to prevent them from being snatched up or carried away by of one them. Man, we had fun out in the wilderness! It was all in how you looked at it. We had to go through lawfully and joyfully. I remember my wife Courtnaye and I, plus our two kids at the time, and several church members went on the riverboat cruise that a lot

of the locals were raving about. And it was awesome! My
wife and I took pictures of the never before seen waterfalls
and watched the wild goats on top of the hillsides. Yeah,
it was quite different from the pelican state of Louisiana.
And granted, we had river cruises in New Orleans, but
something was altogether different about this one. It could
very well have been because of all that we were dealing with
at the time. However, I will say that considering how busy
my wife and I had been back in New Orleans with our
jobs, this time in the wilderness, although tough at times,
allowed us the opportunity to realize just how important
we were to one another. It drew us closer to each other,
our children, our fellow Christian brothers and sisters, but
most importantly, to God."

This trip did bring us a lot closer to each other. Every stop was another
opportunity to grow in relationship with our families, friends, and fellow
church members. But I would echo the fact that God had granted us that
season of time to recognize that most importantly, we needed to develop a
deeper personal relationship with Him so that one day we would be able to
draw others unto His Son Jesus Christ by the word of our testimonies.

That evening after the boat ride and after my wife and I had returned
from being in Austin all day, we received word that there was a brand new
and nearly vacant apartment complex located in Marble Falls. A little later
on that night, my wife and I, along with a few other members, drove over
to check it out. On our way, a local police officer discovered that we were a
little lost and driving slower than the steady flow of traffic. So by all right,
he pulled us over and questioned whether we were we lost and if we needed
help (I'm sure the Louisiana license plates gave us away). We were very
unfamiliar to the area, and so yes, we did need help finding the complex.

The officer kindly jumped back into his cruiser and escorted us straight
to The Vistas Apartments. As we drove around, we could see that the
buildings were definitely new. It seemed to be a nice, clean, community-style
complex tucked away within the Texas hill country. But because it was late
and dark outside, we couldn't see much. So I decided to wait for daylight to

call and schedule an appointment to view the interior of the apartments. We thanked the officer for escorting us and headed back to the lodge.

*   *   *

Well, I called the next morning, and then the waiting began – waiting for a response back from the apartment manager, from the Texas Housing Authority, and from our real estate agent (who had been searching as well). In the meantime, we continued to enjoy our stay as best as we could. I recall one night when we all gathered together for an evening of fellowship and fun at the lodge. I'd agreed to allow our drama ministry, Cross Communications, to host a Christian Night of Comedy in one of the fellowship halls, and I'm glad that I did because it was a night full of extreme laughter! The skits, impromptu exchanges, stand-up comedy, and imitations (especially the children imitating their parents) were absolutely hilarious. Even though the show only lasted a few hours, I think we all slept a little easier that night. It allowed us to escape just for a little while the harsh reality that we were still all *homeless*.

But that was not the only great evening that we had while we stayed at the lodge. Before departing, we had a special dinner celebration giving thanks unto God that I think most of us will never forget. Instead of having our regular dinner in the dining hall, we arranged for a banquet-style buffet in the courtyard and had our meal by the campfire. It was something that we'd never done before, and we thought it would be nice to have everyone, including the retreat staff, come out to enjoy an evening dinner service under the stars.

From the beginning, God's awesome presence was in our midst. There was food, fellowship, fun, and worship. Beth Williams, a local guitarist, came by to play a few free-spirited praise and worship songs. It was a night of joy, celebration, and thankfulness to the Lord for all He had done for us! One of the most memorable songs that our worship leader Erick Brown led us in was called "In Your Glory" by Clint Brown. It's a song that represents resting in God's presence and signifies true worship. We all sang with hands lifted to the Lord in worship and adoration, and, throughout the night, some of our members even danced as an expression of their gratitude.

The Lord had delivered us from the floods, made provision throughout the evacuation process, protected us on the road, and kept us pressing and holding on strong as a ministry. This service was a special token of our appreciation and a wonderful opportunity to give thanks. And, of course, after we ate, sang, and gave thanks, I preached the Word. Overall, I would say that we really enjoyed ourselves that night.

*   *   *

In all, we had stayed at the lodge for only a week when I got the sense that the Lord wanted everyone to move again. In that time, we had been waiting on some form of housing to open up. FEMA was ready to assist most of us financially, but I hadn't received any solid leads for housing yet. I was seeking a place that would accommodate everyone, because this was new territory for us and we wanted to stay together as a church. I'll admit that I was growing a little tired of all the traveling, but I continued to remain hopeful and optimistic, even though I didn't have any answers yet.

As we were preparing to leave, I'll never forget looking up and seeing several bald eagles soaring high in the morning sky. As I watched, it felt as if God were saying to me, "Keep running the race, don't give up. When you are weak, I will make you strong. You won't faint, because I'm going to carry you through on wings of eagles." I immediately thought of Isaiah 40:31, which says, "But they that wait upon the Lord shall renew their strength; they shall mount up with wings as eagles; they shall run, and not be weary; and they shall walk, and not faint."

What the Lord was saying to me through this Scripture was that He was going to be our strength as we waited for Him to fulfill His promises in our lives. He had a purpose for it all. No matter what it looked like on the surface, all I needed to focus on was pressing towards the mark of the high calling (Philippians 3:14). As I continued watching those eagles fly, I rested in the assurance that Psalm 108:4 (NLT) gives us: "For Your unfailing love is higher than the heavens. Your faithfulness reaches to the clouds." He is faithful! I knew He was going to carry us through because He was with us, and also because He knew that we could handle it. God said that He would never put more on us than we could bear (1 Corinthians 10:13). Trenae Thompson recalls how even in the toughest times, God is still with us to carry us through the storms of life:

Trenae

"Before we evacuated for Hurricane Katrina, I was having a bit of a rough stormy season of my own. In the summer months leading up to the storm, the hardcore city streets of New Orleans claimed the lives of three family members whom I held very close to my heart. In June of 2005, my aunt was killed in a violent drive by shooting; in early July, my grandfather was stabbed to death; and in the latter part of July, I received the most devastating and shocking news of my life – my youngest brother was shot and killed. So when the hurricane struck, I was still a little numb from the pain. However, with the aftermath of Hurricane Katrina and seeing how so many people were hurting and scattered about all throughout the country, I sort of forgot what I was feeling inside and began sympathizing and praying for others. After Rita hit and we continued to travel across the state of Texas, I began to realize that the journey was actually helping to take my mind off of what had just recently happened and what *was* happening at the time. I knew that it was nobody but God who was redirecting my thoughts. But then I'll never forget when we were staying in the Canyon of the Eagles, thoughts of my family members began to flood my mind again. For that small moment in my life, I remember feeling so alone and hurt. But that's when the Holy Spirit reminded me that I was not alone, that God was with me, and that this was just *His* way of drawing me closer to Himself. After that, I remember getting into my car and taking a long drive along the curvy hillside road near the lodge. I needed to get away for a moment to talk to Him. I needed to be honest with God. I needed to cry, because I didn't understand the recent deaths, especially my brother's. And as the hot tears rolled down my face, God spoke to me gently, saying, 'My thoughts are not your thoughts, neither are your ways

My ways…' (Isaiah 55:8-9). And in that still moment with God, I received freedom from my pain and a release in my spirit that was far beyond my imagination. The Lord had used the storms in my life to help me not to lean on my own understanding, but to trust that His plan was far better than how I felt. And through this, He taught me how to trust Him more, and to lean on *Him* for comfort, strength, and peace."

Without a doubt, Trenae had been hit hard with a series of unexpected trials that appeared to be totally unbearable, but God never meant for her to go through them alone. He was right there with her the entire time, strengthening and comforting her along the way. And just as He was strengthening Trenae, He was doing the same for all of us who were experiencing the trials of Hurricanes Katrina and Rita.

The tribulations that we experience in this life are tough at times, but they are all preordained. For instance, God knew when and where the hurricanes would strike and that this exodus would shake things up in our spirits, hopefully to draw us closer to Him. He knew that it would bring forth increased faith and deliverance in many of our lives and in the lives of others around us.

We were set apart for this specific journey. And God had already prepared us for success long before the storms made landfall. Jesus was going to make us strong through it all. The Bible assures us in Philippians 4:13, "I can do all things through Christ which strengtheneth me." We just needed to keep trusting in Him while enduring all the way to the end (Matthew 24:13).

And with that being said, it was time for us to get back on the road again. This time we were headed *back* to Austin to stay at the Woodward Hotel and Suites Conference Center.

We stayed at the AmeriSuites for one day. And then
we stayed at the Canyon of the Eagles for about a
week. Before we left, we had dinner by the campfire,
sang praise & worship songs unto the Lord, and above
there I am preaching the Gospel to help strengthen us
for the continued journey. I never stopped preaching.

CHAPTER SEVEN:

Troubled Waters

Austin, Texas

"For we wrestle not against flesh and blood, but against
principalities, against powers, against the rulers of the darkness
of this world, against spiritual wickedness in high places."
Ephesians 6:12

Early in the morning on Thursday, October 13, our church prepared to move onward to its *sixth* destination, the Woodward Hotel and Conference Center in Austin, Texas. I, on the other hand, had a very different trip ahead of me. The same day, I left camp to go to New Orleans with fifteen or so brothers from the church to see if there was anything left to salvage from the church and our homes. I left my wife in charge of the church and arranged for a few of our ministers to assist with any overall needs while I was away, and then the men and I left.

We arrived in New Orleans late in the evening and stayed overnight at the home of one of our church's family members in the uptown area. Early the next morning, we headed to the church and searched for anything we could retrieve and repair, but unfortunately there wasn't much.

In New Orleans, Smoking for Jesus Ministry owned more than just a church building – we also owned the shopping strip mall next door to the church. That was where our three businesses, the Smokehouse Restaurant,

From Glory to Glory Beauty and Hair Salon, and In the Hands of the Master Lawn Care, were located, as well as our church nursery and administrative offices. We also leased out a nail salon for additional church income purposes. I'd say it was a pretty nice establishment…until Hurricane Katrina got a hold of it.

The storm winds had blown so strongly that they had ripped off almost the entire exterior brick wall of the restaurant. That had left a huge gaping hole in the building, which had allowed open access to everything that was inside. With all of the looting that was going on in the city, just about everything was stolen. Nevertheless, I knew that somehow God would provide a way for us to make repairs one day, and possibly even restore the businesses.

But it would be a long time before we could have our buildings fixed up for services or anything else. In the meantime, we just collected and packed up what we could, tried our best to clean up the church and reclaim any items that were recoverable, locked up, and then walked out the doors.

*   *   *

After we'd left the church, we went to my house, which was located about a mile away. When I opened the door to my two-story brick home, I saw that the sofa, chairs, tables, dishes, appliances, you name it, had all been tossed across the entire lower level. And the smell was horrible. I looked up and caught sight of the waterline, which had nearly reached the ceiling (about eight feet high). Sadly, I knew that we'd lost everything downstairs.

As I proceeded upstairs, I was hoping and praying that everything there was dry and untouched by the flood waters. Amazingly enough, *nothing* upstairs had been touched. All of those years of collecting study and teaching materials and resources had not gone to waste – everything had been preserved! Hallelujah!

My wife and I had winter clothes still hanging up dry in the closets, as well as other clothing that was neatly folded and tucked away in drawers… just as we'd left them on that early morning of Sunday, August 28. God knew that it would turn cold during the time of our traveling and that we would need winter clothing (note: all of our summer clothes were downstairs). So He had supplied for our needs once again! We were truly fortunate and blessed.

Once we had gotten everything from the church, strip mall, my house, and a few other members' houses and apartments, we loaded up the U-haul truck and other vehicles to head back to Austin. I was ready to get back to Texas. I had to finalize a place for all of us to live and the kids and teenagers needed to get back into school. Plus, just in case any of the housing facilities or apartment managers called to schedule an appointment, I wanted to be available. I was still waiting for a return call from The Vistas Apartments in Marble Falls concerning the vacancies I'd heard about. So we really needed to get back. I figured that once we'd established ourselves somewhere in Texas, then we could later strategically coordinate plans for the church and the buildings in New Orleans.

*   *   *

When the brothers and I arrived at the Woodward Hotel in Austin on Saturday, October 15, I really didn't know what to expect. Judging from the outside, I couldn't tell much of anything, but once we'd walked inside that establishment, it was another story. Immediately, we realized that we'd entered a whole different world. When we were preparing to leave the Canyon of the Eagles, our initial plan had been to go back to the AmeriSuites, but one of our church member's parents informed us that the Woodward Hotel was a better place. Once I'd arrived, though, I begged to differ. After my initial assessment of the hotel, I knew that we weren't going to be staying there very long.

A lot of hurricane evacuees were staying at this particular hotel, and unfortunately a lot of these young men and women were found smoking, drinking, selling drugs, and cursing profusely inside and outside the hotel. It was rough. Truth be told, it was a very dark place. There was a lot of sin present. Trenae Thompson and Joseph Brown can testify to this:

Trenae

"When we walked into the Woodward Hotel, it looked like the hood. No lie and no offense, but I have to speak

85

honestly. There were a lot of evacuees just hanging around everywhere. Compared to all of the beautiful hotels and retreat centers we'd stayed in over the course of the journey, this place was downright scary and unsafe. Initially, before my husband returned from the trip to New Orleans with our pastor and several other brothers from the church, it was just me and my six month old baby boy. I prayed that the Lord would keep us safe. While we were staying there, I remember this strange guy who would come out of his room and peep by the elevator all the time, almost as if he were scoping us out or something. I don't know. But it was weird. Then, outside of one of the rooms, I noticed this white towel underneath the door. The occupants of the room were trying to keep the weed smoke from seeping outside the room, but that didn't help, because the halls reeked of marijuana and smoke. Aside from all of that, overall, this was really a group of people who were still hurting, displaced, and who didn't have any hope. They were simply doing what they knew to do. And I felt like the devil was whispering in their ears, 'Yeah, go ahead and smoke your life away.' It was different for us. We'd watched the same news reports. We'd lived through the same horrific storm. Yet, we had hope because of Jesus Christ. He was our strength and our Deliverer. Unfortunately, these individuals were still lost and looking for peace and temporary satisfaction through drugs and alcohol. What they really were in need of was the Savior."

Joseph

"When I first stepped foot in the place, I thought maybe we'd stepped on the wrong side of the tracks or something. I really felt like God had put us on the frontline of the battle! I was like, 'God, hast thou forsaken us?' It was one of the roughest hotels that we'd stayed in throughout our journey thus far. It was a hard place. I hadn't seen anything like it in a long time."

I agree. This site was altogether different from the other hotels we had visited. When I first arrived, I rode the elevator to my room on the fourth floor and, when the elevator doors opened, I was instantly greeted with the strong stench of cigarette and marijuana smoke. As I rolled my luggage down the dimly lit hallway, I sensed a definite chill in the atmosphere. I realized then that our enemy Satan was in the building. Our fight here was not against flesh and blood, but against the principalities and rulers in the heavenly realms (Ephesians 6: 12).

The physical realm wasn't all that inviting either. The air in my room felt moist and reeked of mildew, and the furnishings were worn and old. At night, the corridors were noisy with conversations and loud music. There were also many reports of drug activity and smoking in non-smoking rooms, and nearly every time we walked out of our rooms, we heard profanity echoing down the halls. Some of the ladies in our group were even whistled at and mildly harassed in the lobby and hallways.

Cars were also being broken into in the wee hours of the morning. One of our member's family members experienced it firsthand. The thieves stole a mini refrigerator, a microwave, clothes, and some other personal items out of their car. We really needed to remain prayerful and mindful of our surroundings, because it was a rough place.

*   *   *

However unpleasant, the environment in that hotel was not at all unfamiliar to us as a church. Back in New Orleans, we saw this kind of behavior on a regular basis. Our ministry was located on the eastern side of town on Chef Menteur Highway, and those who are familiar with this area know that it has a reputation of drug activity, prostitution, people out at all hours of the night, and loud music booming from passing vehicles. And our church sat right in the heart of it.

At the hotel, I realized that we had walked into a similar environment – just in new territory. Actually, we'd stepped into *spiritual warfare*. We needed to put on our weapons of warfare: The shield of faith, breastplate of righteousness, helmet of salvation, shoes of peace, and the sword of the Spirit (which is the Word of God). The Lord had placed us in the heat of the battle, and I strongly believe that He was testing our faith to see who would give up and who would continue fighting the good fight of faith (1 Timothy 6:12).

I never expected to see this type of activity going on in a hotel, but I believe the Lord wanted to see how we would respond to any situation that He put us in. It's easy to stand when everything's great and the waters are calm, but how about when the waters get rough and troublesome? As far as I could tell, the Lord was definitely testing and proving hearts on this one! We had to push ourselves to not be swayed by attitudes of dismay and fear. We just needed to endure through the testing. The Bible says that those who endure unto the end shall be saved (Matthew 24:13).

During this time, I identified again with the Israelites. Our stay at that particular hotel reminded me of the time when the children of Israel were in the wilderness. They had been staying at a really great place – it had twelve springs and seventy palm trees, and they had been eating and drinking to their hearts' content. Then suddenly things changed, and God took them out of their comfort zone to a place that was dry and rough (Exodus 15:27-16:1).

That's sort of how it was for us. During our visits to Emmanuel Fletcher Church Alive Conference and Retreat Center, Lakeview Baptist Assembly Retreat Center, Holiday Inn Select Hotel, AmeriSuites and the Canyon of the Eagles, everything had seemed great – the food was good, the housing was nice, and the kids were playing. Then, all of a sudden, things shifted. God led us to a very dry place in the form of the Woodward Hotel.

There was no continental or full breakfast every morning or great scenic trails or extraordinary customer service. Instead, we fended for ourselves every morning for food, waded through smoke-filled hallways, and, for the first time, experienced unpleasant hotel management. It certainly seemed to be a desert experience, and in that wilderness situation, God was dealing with our hearts, helping us to align ourselves more fully with His Spirit so that we could *later* receive His blessings (just as He'd done with the Israelites).

*   *   *

Even though we were in an uncomfortable situation, we couldn't take matters into our own hands by mouthing off to people because of the inconveniences of the hotel or in defense of our own personal rights in any way. We needed to stay humble, hold on, and fight against the enemy's tactics through the Word of God. The Bible says in 2 Corinthians 10:4, "For the weapons of our warfare are not carnal, but mighty through God to the pulling down of strong holds."

Some of the things that were going on within the hotel were familiar to some of our members who had once struggled with the strongholds of nicotine, marijuana, drugs, lust, and alcoholism. If we were not careful or strong enough in the Lord, especially with the high level of stress that our displacement laid upon us, some could have potentially been lured back into those old temptations. But with our hearts guarded by the Word of the Lord and our faith steadfast in Him, we held on to the fact that God was mightier than any temptation that threatened our salvation.

Several of our members were being tested in all sorts of ways. For instance, there was a bar in the downstairs lobby, and with something as simple as a microwave, the enemy tried to lure one of our members into his trap. Calvin J. Richard, Jr. describes this occurrence:

Calvin

"My wife and kids needed to eat a hot meal. We had a few cups of Ramen noodles and I needed to heat them up. But the only microwave that was available to us in the hotel (so I thought initially) was located in the bar. And I hadn't been in a bar in years. I knew, though, that going inside was *not* an option for me. And the Holy Spirit helped by prompting me to flee the appearance of evil (1 Thessalonians 5:22). I also figured that if someone saw me walking into that bar who was *not* affiliated with our church, like maybe a guest in the hotel who knew that I was with Smoking for Jesus Ministry, then he or she could've easily thought, 'Hmm, that's one of those church people. And I thought they were saved, but look, he's in the same bar with me.' Examining it from that perspective, I could have potentially killed my witness. So I went to the front desk and asked the clerk if there was another microwave that I could use that was *not* located in the bar. Without question, this particular clerk walked me over to the kitchen, which was closed at the time, to use the microwave in there. So by my yielding to the Holy Spirit, I did not succumb to the devil's trap. James 4:17 says that it is sin to know what you ought to do, and then not do it. Therefore, my family *did* eat a hot meal that night, but it was not due to the microwave in the bar. The Lord created a way of escape."

The devil is very subtle. The Bible warns us with these words: "Stay alert! Watch out for your great enemy, the devil. He prowls around like a roaring lion, looking for someone to devour" (1 Peter 5:8 NLT).

If Calvin hadn't been careful, he could have potentially been snared in a trap, because he did have a past of drinking with friends in sports bars and nightclubs before being saved. Even though there was no desire within him to drink, if he had been weak and vulnerable enough, the enemy could've once again tried to plant those old thoughts and desires in Calvin during those tough times. Thanks to the Lord protecting him, and thanks to his yielding to the Holy Spirit, he was able to escape the trickery of the enemy. "Now all glory to God, who is able to keep you from falling away and will bring you with great joy into His glorious presence without a single fault" (Jude 1:24 NLT).

*   *   *

Due to the temptations that surrounded us, we needed to remain prayerful to stay strong in the Lord. Prayer is a very powerful weapon in spiritual warfare, and we used it quite often. We used it in our rooms, in the parking lot, and even at the storage facility where we were keeping the rest of our belongings from Lumberton and New Orleans. I will never forget gathering together to pray outside of that storage unit. The men and boys assembled together to pray in one area, and the women and girls proceeded to another. The Word tells us to "pray without ceasing" (1 Thessalonians 5:17), so we never stopped praying throughout our travels.

We would come together to pray against the attacks of the enemy regarding strongholds, offenses, temptations, pride, and lust, and we also prayed for strength, faith, endurance, peace, joy, love, and hope. We prayed that we would be a light for others along the way, and that God would give us words of encouragement for those who were going through their own storms in life. 1 Timothy 2:1 (NLT) says, "I urge you, first of all, to pray for all people. Ask God to help them; intercede on their behalf, and give thanks for them."

As we interceded for others and ourselves, we often prayed in the Spirit. We are a body of believers who believe in the power of Holy Ghost and the evidence of speaking in tongues. Praying in the Spirit gave us supernatural strength to press through any given situation. Ephesians 6:18 (NLT) says, "Pray in the Spirit at all times and on every occasion. Stay alert and be persistent in your prayers for all believers everywhere."

Prayer was part of our survival kit. Matthew 18:20 says, "For where two or three are gathered together in my name, there am I in the midst of them."

* * *

The more I thought about it, the more I realized that we had been brought to this particular place for a reason. God is in the business of saving souls 24/7. It didn't take rocket science to figure out that we were at the Woodward Hotel to help win souls for our Lord Jesus Christ. We needed to be light in the midst of darkness. We needed to be the salt and light of the earth. As believers, it is required of us to let our light shine before men so that they may see our good works, and glorify our Father in heaven (Matthew 5:16). In large part, that's what this stop was about, and that's why it was such a fight!

Back in New Orleans, we would go out into the community to witness to people on the streets with the hope of leading them to Christ. And many lives were transformed in those late night encounters on the eastern city street corners. So, while we were staying at the hotel, we reached out to those around us and invited them to our church service in the hotel's main conference room. The service was an incredible opportunity to minister to those who were hurting, and we ministered with the hope that some would come to Christ. Just like every other place God had taken us to, our services saw several guests join us in worship, prayer and fellowship in the Word. And God worked amazing reconciliations throughout our midst! One of our members, Joseph, remembers this:

Joseph

"Before we'd come to the hotel, I hadn't heard from my mom or dad. I actually didn't know if they'd made it out of the city alive. But after getting there, in the hallway, I ended up meeting with my dad for the first time since Hurricane Katrina! It was a divine connection. I told him that my family and I had evacuated with our church, and he informed me that my mom, grandmother, and cousin had made it out safely as well, and that they were all safe upstairs in the hotel room. So immediately I went up to see the rest of my family. It was awesome! Since I knew that our pastor would be preaching that Sunday morning, I invited them all to come to the service. And the next morning, my dad and cousin did actually come, and they both accepted Jesus Christ as their Lord and Savior. That was a blessing to me, but it was also an eye opening experience. In the midst of everything that was going on around us in that hotel, I realized that God had a purpose and a plan for my life. I was able to discover some things concerning His will for me. Through the storm and the journey, I was not only able to reconnect with my family, but God also began to impress upon my heart that I myself needed to draw closer to Him. And that is when I realized that there is nothing more important to me than having a *personal* relationship with Jesus Christ and doing God's will."

Yep! We all have to be about the Father's business through the help of our Lord Jesus Christ and the Holy Spirit. God knows the plans that He has for us. We just have to follow Him. And the further we go, the more He'll reveal to us. Joseph experienced this personally. This trip not only marked a turning point in his life, but in his father's and cousin's lives as well. Sometimes it takes a little rain or a storm to recognize the most important things in our lives. As you can see, souls were saved, set free, and delivered from sin, and spiritual revelation was taking place throughout the journey.

I believe that God sent us that way for *several* reasons. Though it was a little rough and rugged for starters, He was testing our faith and trying the Word that was within us. He knew that we would make it, but *we* had to know that we could make it – through Christ. God will never put more on us than we can bear. He said so in His Word, and God is not a man that He should lie (Numbers 23:19). The Lord always has a purpose and plan for everything that He does. He makes no mistakes. We just have to activate our faith by believing those truths about our God and then live in accordance with His Word.

*   *   *

Well, after service, we made arrangements to check out of the hotel early. Initially, we'd planned on staying there for a month, but I believed and sensed very strongly that our time there was over. At the Woodward, the Lord gave us what we needed (like manna with the Israelites).

He placed a roof over our heads and blessed us with beds to sleep in, and there were fast food establishments nearby. But He didn't stop there. He also gave us the supernatural strength to be lights and witnesses to those who were around us. As a result, during our stay, five lives were saved and God kept us strong in the midst of it all.

I have to mention that during our travels, one of our members purchased a t-shirt for me that read *"Mount Up"* on the front, and on the back, *"Wings of Eagles."* Every time I wore that shirt, my wife and members knew without a shadow of a doubt that we were about to move. And lo and behold, the day had come again when I stood before the congregation with that shirt on.

I remember that day like it was yesterday. I could see the mixed emotions on the faces of my church family when I stood before them wearing that shirt. Some were actually excited, and a few seemed to have question marks painted on their faces. But nonetheless, no one murmured or complained, especially considering where we were at the time. I believe they figured, just like me, that eventually we would settle down somewhere, but as for then it was once again time to *Mount Up*. This time, though, He seemed to be moving us back – back to Burnet, Texas!

This was the shirt I wore just about every time I got up before my members to inform them that we were moving *again* toward God's intended destination for us as a ministry.

Mount Up!

"But they that wait upon the Lord shall renew their strength; they shall mount up with wings as eagles; they shall run, and not be weary; and they shall walk, and not faint."

Isaiah 40:31

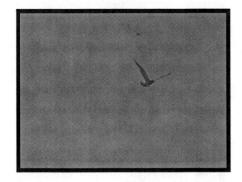

CHAPTER EIGHT:

Raging Waters

Burnet, Texas

"And He arose, and rebuked the wind, and said unto the sea, Peace, be still. And the wind ceased, and there was a great calm. And He said unto them, Why are ye so fearful? How is it that ye have no faith?"

Mark 4:39-40

Well, we made it safely to our *seventh* destination. Praise the Lord for His protection once again! We were now at the Holiday Inn Express located in Burnet, Texas. It was still considered a part of the hill country and was about 11 miles outside of Marble Falls, about an hour away from Austin. Compared to the Woodward, our newest place of habitation felt like heaven.

Walking toward the front doors of the hotel, I noticed that the outside was very well maintained. When I walked inside, a staff member immediately greeted me with a warm and friendly "Hello sir, may I help you?" My wife and I were reasonably familiar with the check-in routine by then, so once we'd squared away the room arrangements, everyone was off to get settled… for what we'd hoped would only be for a little while.

We knew that we would not be going back home to New Orleans anytime soon. There was too much devastation and most of us didn't have any homes left to go back to. So we definitely needed a place to live. By the looks of it, Texas was becoming a more and more likely candidate for our new home state – maybe. At that point, I didn't really know.

All I knew was that we were on a serious faith walk. From my experience, when on a faith walk, everything seems uncertain. It's when your circumstances don't look good or you feel like it's not going to work out. But that's when faith is supposed to kick in. That's when you have to *believe* that everything will in fact work out for your good, even when you can't see with the naked eye. 2 Corinthians 5:7 says, "For we walk by faith, not by sight." That's why I clung to the hope that the Lord would soon settle us down somewhere, maybe even close by. The Bible says that "faith is the substance of things hoped for, the evidence of things not seen" (Hebrews 11:1).

With that being said, I assigned several ministers to watch over our members and help keep order while my wife and I went out to look for more permanent housing. We ended up waiting for days on apartment and housing corporations to call us back with a definite answer to whether or not they could house all of us. In the meantime, my wife and I kicked around the idea of building a subdivision when all of our traveling was done, possibly even in the Cedar Park area (which was only minutes from Austin). We left all options open.

* * *

To help pass the time, we enjoyed the comforts offered by this hotel, especially its continental breakfast, which we enjoyed every morning. Many of our members would come down at their convenience to eat and fellowship, while the kids would come running into the lounge, still in their pajamas, to sit down and enjoy bowls of cereal and sip orange juice with their friends. Some of the moms got together to drink coffee, swap stories, and offer each other support. The men enjoyed the lounge area, where they could be found reading the local newspaper, eating, talking, and watching sports on the big screen television mounted on the wall.

We also arranged with the management to hold our praise and worship services and Bible studies in the hotel's conference room, which worked out perfectly. It's truly staggering how God cleared the way for us to hold services in all of the hotels, retreat centers, and parks that we stayed at.

The Lord also blessed us by allowing us to have our praise team members in attendance, as well as our intercessory team and all of our sound and camera men. The Lord knew that we would need our entire body to stand strong through the raging waters...*together*. He was seriously providing for all of our needs. He is faithful!

When put into the perspective of God's amazing provision, the question of where we would permanently reside became much less of a burden. He was providing for everything else, and I knew that He could and would provide housing at the right time and the right place. It was incredible how He built our faith; all we had to do was look back a few steps to see what He'd already done and believe in His provision for the future. The Bible even reassures us: "I have never seen the righteous forsaken or their children begging bread" (Psalm 37:25 NIV). And with that in mind and in heart, I trusted that we would eventually have a place to call home.

* * *

At this point, our ministry and our members were able to enjoy a lot of down time. Some visited local stores to pass the time, and others hung back at the hotel to relax, exercise, pray, read, and even study. We had a lot of free time. But it hadn't always been like that. At home in New Orleans, we were always busy. Courtnaye Richard expounds on this fact:

Courtnaye

"Before the hurricanes, my husband and I were kept very active by our involvement in the church. There was so much to be a part of! Every third Friday of the month, the women and men would come together for prayer for three hours, every second Tuesday was our women's 'Praise, Worship, and Word' service, every fifth Tuesday was Women's Night; every Saturday was corporate prayer with the entire church body; Wednesday night was our weekly discipleship class; Thursday was Praise Team rehearsal (for me); and on Sundays, we had Sunday school and our Sunday service. My husband was also busy with Monday night men's Bible study, the men's Dance Team, and our drama group, Cross Communications. Not to mention, we shared in many fellowship opportunities such as birthday parties, baby showers, weddings, vow renewals, the marriage refresher, and the like. That was our schedule. And at the time, we both had full time jobs and were raising two kids. So our schedules were pretty busy. Granted, it was hard, but we relied heavily on Jesus to keep us strong. We endured through all of our ministry responsibilities and obligations, and actually had fun in the process! God was teaching us how to become true born-again believers, worshipers of Christ, servants for His kingdom, and so much more. As a result, when the hurricanes came rushing in, our minds remained stable and at peace because our thoughts had been trained to stay fixed on the Lord. Isaiah 26:3 says, 'Thou wilt keep him in perfect peace, whose mind is stayed on thee: because he trusteth in thee.' So even though we'd lost our house, car, and possessions and had to resign from our jobs, we still had God's perfect peace!"

Without a doubt, we had been really busy in ministry. But let me take a moment to make clear that God was not so much concerned about the busyness of our ministry as much as He was interested in our spiritual growth, character, and being a witness to the life of faith through Jesus Christ. That is what ministry is about. In our case, God had been preparing us for the storms ahead and for the history-making journey that would be written in our hearts forever.

*   *   *

As the days went on, I kept my cell phone glued to my side in the hope that something would come through for us concerning housing. Honestly, I was ready for the extended vacation to end and was looking forward to things getting back to normal. Waiting wasn't easy. Trusting God wasn't simple either. But I knew it was best…even when God had become silent again.

Yes, after about a week of staying there, God was silent again. But even still, I had to continue pressing through in faith. During that time, some of our members were growing afraid of where we might settle down. For many, New Orleans was all they had known. Some of them never had any hopes or dreams of ever leaving the city. And here they were wandering around in strange places, not knowing what the next day would hold for them. Most were simply trying to hold onto the faith that they did have, but even that could sometimes be difficult.

A few of them were also becoming puzzled and anxious. We were running low on money, and people wanted to know what God was doing. I didn't know everything, and I wasn't pushing down any doors to make something happen. I certainly wasn't about to mess up and strike the rock like Moses did.

We were at a point when we simply couldn't rely on our feelings; instead, we had to rely on our faith in God. We were all experiencing the effects of these storms together. We were not alone. And God had not forgotten us. He was still on the throne, watching everything that was transpiring in our lives. Knowing that, we just needed to keep trusting in the Lord until we'd reached the end of our stormy journey.

However, I knew what was happening. The waves of fear, doubt, and weariness had begun to stir up again and kick against the hearts of our members. God specializes in storms, and in the midst of them, He tracks our progress. I believe that He was trying to draw us closer to Him to increase our faith while allowing us to encounter His immeasurable peace.

The Lord didn't want us to go inward, but instead He wanted us to steal away to Him and recognize that He was in absolute control. When Jesus' disciples were afraid in the midst of the storm, Jesus "arose, and rebuked the wind, and said unto the sea, Peace, be still. And the wind ceased, and there was a great calm. And He said unto them, Why are ye so fearful? How is it that ye have no faith?" (Mark 4:39-40).

The disciples had allowed fear to grip their hearts so much that they lost the faith that they once had because of what they saw happening around them. The sea was raging, Jesus was there, but they were still afraid. They didn't think that they would make it safely through to the other side. But Jesus was in control, and He brought peace in the midst of their storm.

* * *

No storm could ever measure up to the peace of God. I've recognized over the years that when we experience His peace, our thoughts are clear and there's no worry or doubt. It's as though nothing else around you really matters. And it's not as if there's nothing happening, because there is, but what really matters is how we deal with it.

Unfortunately, when times get hard, emotions can rob us of God's peace. In the past, I had preached messages to my members that as Christians, it is okay to be honest with God if you're feeling depressed, angry, uncertain, or saddened by some event or tragedy in life. He knows that we'll experience these emotions. Actually, He is very well aware of them before they are ever felt or whispered in our prayers to Him. But that's when we can be comforted by Philippians 4:7: "And the peace of God, which passeth all understanding, shall keep your hearts and minds through Christ Jesus."

Although most of us were now homeless for the first time in our lives and didn't know where we were going next, God didn't want any of us to dwell or worry about the troubles or circumstances that surrounded us. Paul said in 2 Corinthians 4:8 (NLT), "We are pressed on every side by troubles, but we are not crushed. We are perplexed, but not driven to despair."

When I came to a moment of uncertainty during our long journey, I chose to trust God for everything. I had to lay aside everything that I was feeling on the inside, and refocus on the fact that God had not brought us that far to leave us. He was not going to abandon us. He wanted us to fall back on Him and trust that Jesus, His Son, was going to comfort us and see us completely through to a safe place.

* * *

I figured that I would get a call from one of the apartment complexes sooner or later. But I was also careful not to leak any information until I had all of the facts. I never went before the people unprepared. I always sought the Lord for His Word first. It was too critical of a time, and I didn't want to give anyone false hopes. So I continued to wait…in faith, hope, expectancy, and in His peace.

By this time, we had been staying at the Holiday Inn Select for about two weeks. We needed to get our kids and teens back into school, so I requested that our church nurse, Anitra Torns, get the immunization record waiver forms for them to enroll, which all of the schools had on hand just in case they received any evacuees from New Orleans. Within a matter of days, nearly all of the kids were back in school. Anitra really was a great help in that effort.

It was wonderful seeing the kids get back to a bit of normal life. The rest of us were still waiting for that luxury. I continued to watch and listen very closely for fresh direction from the Lord. I knew that God had something great in store for us…if we could just hold on and wait for His promises, if we could just keep in the forefront of our minds that God is faithful! At that time, we couldn't believe in what we could see; we had to depend on the Lord and fall back on what His Word said. And *we* needed to remain faithful. It was required of us to keep the faith and praise Him through the entire process. The Lord had removed the spirit of heaviness and replaced it with a garment of praise (Isaiah 61:3)!

Shortly thereafter, the time came when God opened the floodgates of heaven and poured us out a blessing! The Vistas Apartments in Marble Falls finally called us back and confirmed their vacancies. We later learned that one of the managers had been praying for over a year for the complex to be occupied because it had been vacant for so long. In God's answer to us, He also answered that manager's prayer.

In mid-October of 2005, we prepared to move into our new apartments. This time, we would finally have places to call our own. Immediately, we sent families to go in and take care of their housing paperwork. FEMA was able to pay for most of our housing, which was a huge blessing.

God had blessed us once more! We had reached the end of our traveling. He'd brought us safely through the journey together. That moment reminded me of a song that we used to sing in the men's Bible study called "If the Lord Had Not Been on Our Side." In the song, the singers express how, if the Lord had not been on their side, all of the raging waters would have swept over them and would have swallowed them alive. Well, God was with us, and He was definitely on our side. He kept us through it all.

We could now rest in the fact that we had a place to once again call home. It was time to *Mount Up* again, because we were now headed to The Vistas Apartments!

Above was the front entrance of the Holiday Inn Express in Burnet, Texas. We stayed there for several weeks before moving to Marble Falls. Below is the hotel lobby and continental breakfast room.

CHAPTER NINE:

After The Rain

Marble Falls, Texas

"Faithful is He Who is calling you [to Himself] and utterly trustworthy, and He will also do it [fulfill His call by hallowing and keeping you]."
1 Thessalonians 5:24 (AMP)

Finally! The Lord had landed us safely. We arrived at The Vistas Apartments in Marble Falls, our *eighth* and final destination. God had answered our prayers, and we finally had a place that we could call home, somewhere to settle down. It reminded me of the story of Noah and the ark – it felt like we'd finally docked. It was like the rain had stopped pouring down in our lives, the water had receded, and we were able to get out of the boat to walk on dry ground. The Lord had carried us through it all, just as He'd promised. And we were off to a fresh start – a new beginning!

Marble Falls is a beautiful, quaint little town. It's known as a retirement community and a great place to take a vacation. The town's slogan is "For a Weekend or For a Lifetime." For some, it's a place to rest after working for many years in the corporate world, and for others, an area to relax during the holidays and summer months. But for us and the locals, it was home.

After settling in, we explored the area and discovered many lake view and waterfront retirement homes, as well as ranches. We learned that the town is known for its beautiful lakes, hills, moderate weather, vast golf courses, festivities, and recreational activities. And we soon found the popular breakfast spot that many locals spoke highly of – the Blue Bonnet Café. We also discovered Main Street, which hosts an array of specialty shops and restaurants. The town was very welcoming, and we were very happy to be there.

We were just excited to finally have somewhere to call home. But, as you can see, Marble Falls was much different from the city life that we were accustomed to. It took us aback for a while because we weren't used to so much quiet. We were used to high rise buildings, highway traffic, busy business districts, and sirens from ambulances and police cars screaming down our streets during all hours of the day and night. We were used to city lights and a faster-paced life. Marble Falls was nothing of the sort. It was much slower and much more peaceful, which I believed we would eventually become accustomed to and enjoy. But initially, we needed to press past the culture shock.

Even though we were from a different place, we found once again that God's goodness in people's hearts is universal. The community folks were very friendly and welcoming, and for that, we were very grateful. Moreover, we were relieved and thankful to finally get off the road. We had found a wonderful temporary homestead in the hill country.

* * *

The apartments were nearly brand new, and everyone was really excited to move in. They'd anticipated this day for a long time. Some moved in sooner than others, depending on the kind of apartment each family needed and could afford. Meanwhile, other members stayed back at the hotel until all of their paperwork was approved and accommodations were arranged. Once everything went through, they received their keys and entered their new apartments.

My wife and I didn't move into our apartment right away because we wanted to make sure that everyone else was squared away first. In the meantime, we met a very kind Christian woman by the name of Kathleen Elliott who was a member of the United Methodist Church in Marble Falls. She lived about fifteen minutes away in an area called Horseshoe Bay.

We first met her at a town meeting in late October, and she later came over to the apartment complex to introduce herself to everyone. In her mid-sixties, this friendly Christian Caucasian woman explained to us that she had been intrigued by our story from the moment she first heard that we were Hurricane Katrina evacuees from New Orleans.

A frequent traveler herself, she took a great interest in us and how we as a church had traveled after the storm. She had just returned from a trip of her own when the Lord led her to us, and she generously offered me and my wife a place to stay at her three-story lake view home. We gladly accepted her invitation.

Her house sat right on the shoreline of Lake LBJ in Horseshoe Bay, and not only was the view incredible, but the interior of her home was beautiful as well. It was so cozy and relaxing, almost like a cottage-style bed and breakfast. She had antique furniture throughout the living and dining room areas and a wall covered with mirrors. Bibles, crosses, Christian artifacts, and reading material were welcoming accents throughout the house. But I want to add here that the focal point in her house was the open Bible that sat next to a narrow wall near the kitchen, where an antique lamp illuminated the Word of God. She explained to us that she leaves the light on 24/7 beaming over this particular Bible, because it is a constant reminder of how God's Word is a lamp unto her feet and how it directs her path. My wife and I agreed that her home felt like a safe haven, especially after everything we'd gone through.

There was also a balcony overlooking the lake itself, which was certainly inviting, but at that point it was cold outside, so we remained indoors. The first night, after we'd gotten settled in and washed up a bit, my wife and I headed straight for bed. We were exhausted. I guess we were so tired from all of the traveling that we just crashed. We really needed to catch up on some much anticipated rest.

For the next couple of weeks, we enjoyed Ms. Kathleen's hospitality. On some mornings, all three of us would have breakfast together and talk. During the day, my wife and I would check in on our members to see how they were acclimating to the new area. We also continued to work with our real estate agent to help us in our search to possibly purchase or build homes in Marble Falls. Some of our members' homes had been completely destroyed in the hurricane, and others had anticipating buying a home before we evacuated. So since we were getting off to a fresh start, we were looking for land to build new homes upon.

At night, my wife and I would relax by reading, resting, or watching television. Sometimes we'd pull back the curtains from the sliding glass door of our lower lodge of the house and watch the waters peacefully lap against the shore.

Ms. Kathleen helped us tremendously by extending her hospitality and home to us. We definitely appreciated her faith, love, and kindness. The Bible says, "So you see, faith by itself isn't enough. Unless it produces good deeds, it is dead and useless. Now someone may argue, 'Some people have faith; others have good deeds.' But I say, 'How can you show me your faith if you don't have good deeds? I will show you my faith by my good deeds'" (James 2:17-18 NLT). Ms. Kathleen truly put her faith into action and showed tremendous love to me, my wife, and our church.

*   *   *

After staying at the lake house for three weeks, my wife and I were finally able to move into our apartment. It was new, modern, and had two bedrooms just for us. When we walked inside, I could still smell the fresh paint on the walls. As I spoke to my wife, I could hear the echo from my voice bounce off the walls of the empty rooms – the *very* empty rooms. We didn't have any furniture.

It didn't take long before I took notice that we all needed the bare essentials to get us started. So, of course, Wal-Mart was the place to go. As the days went on, I remember many of us spent countless hours in Wal-Mart and neighboring community stores stocking our refrigerators with food and gathering up everything else you can think of: pots and pans, plates, bowls, silverware, sheets, comforters, pillows, air mattresses, towels, curtains, bathroom essentials, and other household necessities. But we couldn't buy too much. We still needed to be wise in our spending, because no one had jobs yet.

We needed to look into getting jobs for everyone who was in need of work. A lot of the mothers, though, especially those with small children, weren't quite ready to go back to work. Some who had worked full time back in New Orleans had discovered over the course of our journey that they were being called to spend more time with their children and be more available to help their husbands. So they took advantage of the break from Corporate America! In the meantime, I, my wife, and a couple of interested members put together a committee specifically designed to help men and singles find employment.

I'll admit that jobs didn't come easy or right away. Many of our members had to wait awhile for something to open up, and the fact that we were in a smaller town meant that there were fewer jobs to go around. Meanwhile, everyone registered for food stamps, and FEMA was still helping us to pay rent. Most of us were still sleeping on air mattresses or newly purchased comforter sets. We didn't have much, but we learned quickly how to be content with what we had.

Paul said in Philippians 4:11-12 (NLT), "Not that I was ever in need, for I have learned how to be content with whatever I have. I know how to live on almost nothing or with everything. I have learned the secret of living in every situation, whether it is with a full stomach or empty, with plenty or little." And with that *contentment*, God moved on our behalf. Next thing we knew, the community came together to help us out!

*   *   *

Once the community of Marble Falls and the surrounding counties got word that a large group of Hurricane Katrina evacuees were staying at The Vistas Apartments, hundreds of people came by week after week to bring us donations. Churches, organizations, families, and individuals donated items to us and extended a helping hand. They brought everything from bed sets and mattresses to sofa and dinette sets, along with other things like sheets, curtains, bathroom essentials, and clothing. Different individuals came by and brought over washers and dryers. Before it was all over, every household had a set. God was providing in abundance once again! His Word says in Philippians 4:19, "But my God shall supply all your need according to His riches in glory by Christ Jesus."

We were so grateful! And as more donations poured in weekly, we had to put together a committee to make sure that everyone had what they needed for their homes. As a church and as a body of believers, we continued to look out for each other. Obadiah Williams further explains:

Obadiah

"Initially, I was not a member of the church. I was only 17 years old at the time of the evacuation for Hurricane Katrina, and before that happened, I was really not interested in going to church. Sure, my brother Simeon Williams (who was and still is a member at Smoking for Jesus Ministry) would call me periodically and invite me to the church, but I would always turn him down and say, 'Maybe some other time.' Well, no doubt, that time had finally come. I couldn't run away from God anymore. The storm came and caused me to experience the Lord for myself through the members of my brother's church. Immediately, I was able to see firsthand the move of God in the midst of the circumstances. Through the journey, the Lord provided food, shelter, clothes, and fellowship like I'd never seen before in my life. And I saw for myself true men and women of God working and dwelling together in unity. The members were truly sel*fless*. For example, when someone didn't have something, others were willing to give the shirt off their backs or shoes off their own feet to satisfy the needs of another. I saw Christians who really considered others higher than themselves. Frankly, that was big for me to see. God showed me people who really loved Him and believed in His Son. And to think, looking back before the storm, I was not even searching for Jesus. But He was looking for me. And as a result of the hurricanes, my brother, and the members of this church, I have since then accepted Jesus Christ as my Lord and Savior. And I can honestly say, accepting *His* invitation was the best decision that I could've ever made."

It was great seeing everyone pull together and help one another out in a time of crisis. I am most grateful that Obadiah was able to see for himself the awesome hand of God moving through people, and, most importantly, that he accepted the Lord Jesus Christ as his personal Savior.

*   *   *

As time went on, the Lord continued to build greater unity within our church and a sense of community within our ministry. We were now all living around each other and getting to know one another even better. Many were excited that they were neighbors. Friendships and relationships that had been forged during our journey continued to grow long after our traveling ended.

At home in New Orleans, our members would get a chance to see each other at church or at different fellowships, of course, but now God allowed us to see each other more often around the apartment complex. And I have to say that it was nice to see the kids playing together on the playground, and parents getting together to fellowship more. It was a fresh start for everyone.

Even though our families now had places to live, we still didn't have a church home. I figured once we'd gotten settled into our apartments, I could begin searching for a new building to house our services. In the meantime, we took turns each week conducting Bible studies inside members' apartments.

We still needed to have church, because we were still in fact a ministry. And most importantly, we needed to continue growing in the Lord. I remember the women continued their Tuesday morning Bible study on the book *Drawing Near* by John Bevere. They'd started the study in New Orleans before the hurricane, and God had seen fit to resume the lesson in Marble Falls. And what an appropriate time to do so! Most of the ladies now had time available to really dig into the study.

Interestingly, the illustration on the cover of the book was a picture of hills, mountains, lakes, and trees, an image which closely resembled our newfound residence. The lesson was also perfect for where we were at the time in our walk with the Lord. I believe that part of the reason why God brought us way out into the hill country was not only to bless us, but because He wanted to draw us closer to Himself. He was calling all of us to draw near to Him. The Scripture James 4:8 reminds us: "Draw nigh to God, and He will draw nigh to you."

God was drawing us into a deeper and more intimate relationship with Him. And He used the storms to navigate us straight to His heart. I believe that He was trying to take us to a higher place in Him…a higher level of intimacy…a higher connection. It wasn't about church as usual, but about knowing Him deeper through prayer, fasting, seeking Him diligently through His Word, and truly representing His Son Jesus Christ in a greater capacity. That's why it was important that we go through the entire process, whatever that process proved to be in the end. I believed with everything within me that this was only the beginning of greater things to come.

*   *   *

God continued to provide for our needs as a church. Even though we didn't have an actual building, He opened up many doors within the community to maintain our weekly prayer meetings and services. One location that we used quite a bit for our Sunday services was a pavilion in Johnson Park, where many people came to visit and fellowship with us. Some even accepted Christ as their Lord and Savior. Wherever we went, we had an altar call. No matter the weather, whether indoors or outdoors, the invitation to Christ was always made available to anyone and everyone. And if anyone had special prayer needs, we prayed for them as well. We didn't turn anyone away.

Sometimes we conducted our corporate prayer meetings in the park, in the parking lot at the apartments, or in local churches. Many of the churches in the area knew that we were a ministry without a building and that we were hurricane evacuees, so they allowed us to utilize their facilities free of charge. That was a blessing. God provided places where we could come together to worship Him, dance in His presence, fellowship, and receive His Word on a consistent basis. That is what mattered most.

*   *   *

After a month of having our Sunday services at the local churches, we moved into the Marble Falls High School cafeteria. It was convenient for us because it was right up the road from our apartments. It was also indoors and spacious. Once word got out that we were having our services there, people from outside of our church came to visit us week after week. We even had our vow renewal service there one weekend.

One rainy Sunday morning in late November, two of our members from the women's dance ministry danced to the song "Don't Give Up on Jesus" by Darryl Coley and Vanessa Bell Armstrong. This song and dance perfectly outlined the entire history of our travels. This particular interpretive dance is one that most of us will always remember. Stacy Brown, one of the dancers, explains what happened:

Stacy

"It was overcast that early Sunday morning in November of 2005. I remember it like it was yesterday. The sky was partially gray, but as the raindrops fell against the Marble Falls High School cafeteria windows, I felt like the rain and the gray sky were physical representations of what many of us felt on the inside. The Praise Team had just finished singing their last worship song, and many in the room had begun to cry. The atmosphere was thick and the overall emotion in the room was somber...I believe it was because even though we had come to a place of safety and temporary rest, we still had vivid memories of the many lives lost during the storm, and some had family members scattered throughout the country...some of which were my own. I hadn't heard from my mom or two brothers yet and I didn't know if they were dead or alive. And Sister Travonda had just lost her mother to a tough battle of endometrial cancer. So it was really hard for us. Nevertheless, we took our positions to minister in dance even though we ourselves were heavy in spirit. The stage was set with props that represented every stop we had made in our traveling. And, for a few moments, we relived it all again. As the music played, we fought through every emotion that was going on inside of our bodies so that God would freely use us to encourage His people and ourselves *not to give up.* And while keeping everything into perspective and portraying the vision of our travels and song, we simply free flowed. After the dance, I cried. I felt so empty inside, and had poured out and given all of myself in that dance. I had nothing left but to cry and worship! That was the first time that many of us saw our pastor cry – the first time since he had begun to lead us through the wilderness, guided by the Lord, bringing us closer to the promises that God had in store for us all. God had given us that moment to grieve, but we knew that we couldn't stay there on that cold, hard floor too long. No, we had to get up and keep moving, and remember just what the song said: 'For He's met all your needs before and you dare not doubt, He'll bring you out…When you've tried everything you know and you're looking for a place to go, don't give up on Jesus.'"

It was a defining moment. It was as though God was speaking to us through the words of the song by telling us, "Don't give up." We couldn't rely on our emotions and what surrounded us; instead, we had to keep pressing forward while continuing to rely on the Holy Spirit to lead and guide us as we held on to the promises of God.

*   *   *

After a few months went by, many of our members found jobs. With that accomplishment under our belts, we agreed as a church to organize a fundraiser to help raise money for our church families who had not yet received financial assistance from FEMA. Not only that, we also wanted to give back to the community of Marble Falls and the surrounding areas for helping us when we'd first arrived.

We talked about putting on a great big festival, and once we'd agreed on the overall idea, we put together a planning committee, partnered with the Texas Housing Foundation, and gained approval to house the event at the First Baptist Church. And immediately, we got to work on it! The planning took a lot of hard work and effort, but with the Lord's grace and a dedicated team, we were able to get it all done in time. On Saturday, February 25, 2006, "Hill Country New Orleans Style" began!

People came out from everywhere! Over 1,400 people showed up for the event. Men, women, and children came out to enjoy the food and festivities. We served hot bowls of real New Orleans style gumbo, red beans and rice, jambalaya, seasoned fried fish, barbecue, fried chicken, macaroni and cheese, potato salad, hamburgers and hot dogs, iced tea, and soft drinks. As people stood in line waiting for their Louisiana cuisine, they were also able to view a huge table display of our journey throughout Texas.

We provided more than just food – we had a lot of fun too! For the kids, we had a moonwalk, a dunk tank, face painting, pony rides, basketball, family games, and arts and crafts. Our Praise Team sang praise and worship songs, our dance ministries danced, and the kids sang and rapped Christian songs as well. It was a lot of fun! Through this event, we did more than just show our thanks to the incredible folks who had helped us – we also established a unique presence in our new community.

Everyone who came out had a great time, and people had the option of donating toward our cause. Every single contribution given that day was used toward rent for our church members who had not received their rental assistance from FEMA, so even as we thanked the community for helping us, they helped us again in return.

After the "Hill Country New Orleans Style" event, we received many compliments on the festivities and especially on the food. Since the cuisine had generated so much interest and seemed to be in high demand, we looked into opening a restaurant in the area. It was a really exciting possibility, and we hoped we could start a restaurant again. Of course, all of our supplies and appliances had been lost, but we knew God could provide.

Our search began and, thirteen miles from Marble Falls in a town called Round Mountain, God provided in a mighty way! A restaurant facility was up for rent and it came with everything that we needed to run the business. The owner offered everything to us at an affordable monthly price, and the kitchen and restaurant came fully furnished. All we needed to do was move in. In June of 2006, we officially opened the Real New Orleans Style Restaurant, and we were able to employ over twenty of our members and enjoyed the blessing of about ten volunteers. God had moved once again! And the community flocked week after week to enjoy our New Orleans cuisine and Louisiana-style cooking.

Local newspapers began running stories not just about our journey and the hurricane, but also about how our lives were being rebuilt there in Marble Falls. Austin's KVUE news reporter, Olga Campos, even came all the way out to cover stories on us as well, which included the opening of (and a few samples from) our new restaurant.

* * *

All of the excitement with the new restaurant was great, but it didn't lessen the reality that we were still in need of a permanent place to fellowship. God had blessed us abundantly in Marble Falls, and He wasn't finished with us yet.

I thought back to when we were in New Orleans, months prior to Hurricane Katrina, when our church went on a three-day fast. The purpose of that fast was to seek the Lord to provide the funding to build our new church on less than an acre of land across the street from the existing structure we'd purchased. Of course, those plans fell through after the hurricane. But we still believed that God would someday honor our sacrificial prayers according to His perfect will for a new church.

In Marble Falls, we had a real estate agent looking for places for us, but after months of searching, nothing really turned up. We also considered buying the vacant land across the street from The Vistas Apartments, but we never could come to a mutual financial agreement with the owners. It was extremely out of our price range.

Finally, after months of looking for property, one of the brothers in our church, Darron Woods, got word that the owner of the Old Buckner's Boys Ranch in Burnet was looking to sell his property. Clearly, we were in dire need of a permanent building to house our many services, ministerial events, prayer meetings, and church functions. By that time, our ministry had already exhausted all of our resources at the First Baptist Church, First Assembly of God, the Methodist Church, and the Marble Falls High School. We were a pretty sizeable group, and things were getting rather tight. It became hard for us to conduct our normal ministerial responsibilities, engagements, and events because of space and availability.

We were thrilled with the possibility presented by the ranch, so we gave the owners, Mr. and Mrs. Teeples, a call. My wife remembers what happened next:

Wife Claudette

"After talking to Mr. Teeples, my husband and I took a ride to visit the ranch to see if it was something that we would be interested in leasing or buying. Upon meeting with him, he told us that he knew it was ordained by God to sell the ranch, because for years it was hard for him to sell it due to many deed restrictions. But after years of no potential buyers, they were finally given one year to sell it. And so that's when he and his partners came together on August 29 to pray that God would send someone to buy the property within a year's time. Well, lo and behold, their prayer was petitioned the day of Hurricane Katrina's landfall. I need to also mention that there was a caretaker on the ranch who was also interested in buying the land, but he wasn't quite ready yet. He'd taken care of the grounds himself very well, so much so that if we did decide to purchase it, we didn't have much to do upon moving in. But the weird part about it was that he told us that he wanted it and that he too, had been praying about it. He also wanted to pray with us, that whomever God chose to give it to, it would be His will. So we agreed to pray with him, but I was like, 'Lord, just give it to him, because we don't want to come here and take anything from anyone.' Plus the place was three million dollars, and we were concerned that we wouldn't be able to make the down payment. But after praying about it and seeking the Lord in prayer, God answered. It was settled. The Lord had decided that the land was ours! And a little while later, Mr. Teeples worked in the agreement that he would only charge us $10 a month, just to show that we did have a lease agreement. We hoped to go to closing in August 2006 (which didn't officially happen until January of 2007). Nonetheless, we had agreed to the terms, and he met his deadline. But most importantly, we now had a place that we could finally call our *church* home. God is faithful!"

I realized at that moment more than ever before that the Lord was showing us some serious favor in the hill country. But that wasn't even the best part. It was not only one, two, or three acres of land that God had given us – He saw fit to bless us with 56 acres of land!

When we accepted the terms of agreement to purchase the ranch, we decided to divide up the land for different purposes. Part of it would be used for the church and the other part would be left available for any of our members who would like to build homes on the land. There were buildings for our singles ministries, and there were four other houses on the property that we would soon rent out to members who were able and ready to move closer to the church.

The property also housed a huge gym, tennis court, baseball field, cafeteria, administrative building, picnic area by the lake, and even room to build a swimming pool and a playground later. Most importantly for us, a previous ministry had built a beautiful church building with a large sanctuary, bathrooms, offices, and classrooms on the land. Praise be to God! We now had a permanent place to worship and serve the Lord.

There is absolutely no limit to what God can do when we sacrifice our lives and seek Him sincerely. He simply does what He wants, when He wants, and for whom He wants. And we received His special favor and blessings. It brought me back to our fast in New Orleans. We'd fasted for three days for nearly *one* acre, and after traveling around to eight different places in obedience to His will, God blessed us with 56 acres of land! He'd honored our fast to so much greater of a degree than we'd ever imagined!

We now had our own church home in Burnet, Texas, which is on the border of Kingsland, about seventeen miles from Marble Falls. It was indeed a new beginning! God is great and worthy to be praised!!! He is faithful! To God be the glory, forever and forevermore!

This is our worship leader, Minister Erick Brown and praise
team ministering to the people in praise and worship early
one Sunday morning service in November 2005. We didn't
have a church *home* yet, so we had service in Johnson Park
in Marble Falls.

Here are Minister Stacy Brown and Travonda Woods dancing to the song, "Don't Give Up on Jesus"; below is Tiffany Thomas, Viola Chapman, and Wendy Armour weeping after dance and giving thanks unto God for bringing us through the storm.

This is The Vistas Apartments where we resided when
we first landed in Marble Falls, Texas.

This was our *Hill Country New Orleans Style* event, where over 1,400 people attended. We showed our appreciation to the community of Marble Falls, Burnet, and surrounding counties for their generosity and hospitality. There was dancing, singing, Christian rapping, games, food, and more!

Above are our restaurant and staff members of The Real
Orleans Style Restaurant in Round Mountain, Texas.
Below was our ribbon cutting ceremony of our newest
restaurant in Marble Falls.

We also own *A Lil Taste* of The Real
New Orleans Style Restaurant
(takeout orders)
which is located in Burnet, Texas.

CHAPTER TEN:

Following in His Footsteps

Burnet, Texas

"And when they had brought their ships to land,
they forsook all, and followed Him."
Luke 5:11

The Lord had answered our prayers! After He'd carried us on wings of eagles through the storms and guided us through *eight* different places within the state of Texas, the Lord landed us on solid ground. We had our own church! It was time to move on and follow through on God's plan to start anew and continue our ministry in Burnet, Texas. I knew that it was the Lord because we'd prayed about it and the Lord had answered us in so many ways. One sign of the Lord's direction was the incredibly favorable agreement that Mr. Teeples made with us for the ranch, and another sign was the size of our current living spaces – they were just too small.

After our trips to New Orleans, our church members had to store our rescued items anywhere we could. My wife and I didn't have enough room in our apartment to house everything we'd brought, which meant I had to store many of my teaching resources and other items in closets, drawers, desks, other members' apartments, and nearby storage facilities because there wasn't enough room. Having everything scattered about can be pretty stressful, and I was definitely feeling it, especially when I had to gather materials to prepare my lessons.

That's when I made the decision to move my wife, myself, and the members of the House of Leah and the House of Joseph into the vacant housing on the ranch. This was one of our first steps to returning to the way things had been in New Orleans. Those houses were a part of the vision that God had given me when I first started the ministry, and I wanted to keep them going.

With that being said, we needed to break our leases with The Vistas Apartments. Management took it pretty well since they had known something like this could happen when we'd moved in. Plus, we'd followed all of the standard procedures within our leases as tenants, so there weren't any problems at all.

*   *   *

Our moving day finally arrived! It was a steaming hot day in July when the U-haul truck arrived to move me and my wife. Several of the brothers from church came over to help us move all of our furniture, clothes, and teaching materials out of the apartments and storage facilities. I never realized how much stuff we had accumulated in almost a year's time. God had blessed us abundantly. And now we were headed towards Burnet.

When we got to the ranch, it felt so good to finally have somewhere to call home again. Even though it was dormitory-style housing, we were thankful. We knew that it would serve as temporary housing, because my wife and I were still planning on building a new house. But for the time being, the Lord had provided more space for us, which allowed me to house all of my teaching resources and study materials under one roof.

After our members in the House of Leah and the House of Joseph had also settled in, our church body began mentally and physically making the transition from New Orleans to Burnet. Meaning, we settled on the fact that the Lord had moved us into a new place, and that we wouldn't be returning to the location we had known as home. Our mourning was cut short, though, by the realization that with new beginnings come new blessings. And God had certainly been blessing us!

The land that He had bestowed upon us was so beautiful. I planned a day for all of the members to come by to see the land for themselves. Some of the looks on their faces were expressions of amazement, shock, and awe! We serve an awesome God! We had to give Him praise. It was a reality! We finally had a church home again.

The Lord saw fit to bless us here for His special purposes, and we were all overjoyed! It seemed only right to hold a church dedication ceremony to give our thanks to God formally for leading us through the storms to our new church home in Texas.

* * *

The first day that we opened the church doors, I was filled with overwhelming emotions. I'll never forget it. I just felt so grateful, blessed, and in awe because of all that God had done for us during the entire journey. He had this land, this ranch, this acreage tucked away just for us. It was all according to His plan. The Holy Spirit brought back to my remembrance Jeremiah 29:11 (NIV) in which the Lord says, "For I know the plans I have for you…plans to prosper you and not to harm you, plans to give you hope and a future."

He definitely had a plan and a future for us – one that we would have never imagined. In 2005, I never would've thought or dreamed that we would ever be in Burnet, Texas. At that point, I had no idea where this place even was. We never looked for it, because we never had a reason to. But when Hurricanes Katrina and Rita struck, our lives were changed forever.

Before the storm, some people had misplaced their faith, some were completely lost, and others were drifting away from the things of God. But God used this storm in mighty ways! Curnara Green, who had not been a member of our church before Hurricane Katrina, is a great example of this. At the age of 22, she had experienced great sorrow after losing her mom to a long battle of colon cancer. Then along came the hurricane, and although she and her three-year-old daughter found a place to stay in Atlanta, spiritually she still felt like she'd drifted out into deep waters, far away from the Lord. But thank God that her younger brother Rodrick Green, who became a member during our travels, threw her a life raft that not only saved her soul, but her young daughter's soul as well. Curnara explains her deliverance in these words:

Curnara

"After my mom died, I sort of lost faith and resented God. I couldn't understand why He would do such a thing by taking my mother away from me. I took care of her when everyone else was doing their own thing. I sacrificed my life to help her. We grew up in the church and my dad is a pastor. So, surely, I thought the Lord would heal her... that He wouldn't let her die. She was a faithful Christian woman who loved the Lord and helped others no matter what. She never gave up believing God...even through her struggle with cancer. But at 50 years old, my mother took her last breath and the battle was over. She'd gone on to be with the Lord. But *I* on the other hand became bitter. I figured that if God would allow this to happen, then He didn't love me anymore. So I thought, 'Why should I serve Him?' It didn't make much sense to me then. After that, I went back into a life of sin. I knew better, but I had lost my hope and faith. And then the storm came. My daughter and I had to evacuate. We headed to Atlanta, and, after the storm, I saw the devastation in New Orleans and decided to start our lives over in Georgia. It wasn't long after that when my younger brother Rodrick called me with an urgent message. He said, 'I believe the Lord is telling me to tell you to leave Atlanta and come out to Marble Falls.' Initially, I thought he was crazy, because I had just begun the process of opening up and running a new restaurant in Atlanta, but shortly thereafter, things started going wrong, and then my car caught on fire one day, my friends were doing crazy stuff, everything was beginning to turn for the worst in my life. So something in me knew that my brother was telling the truth, because

I had been praying that God would give me direction. I needed real answers, because I was lost. I needed help. So due to all of the problems, I turned to the Lord again. And after the call, I prayed and packed up my bags and within three days, my daughter and I were in Marble Falls. In a Sunday morning service there, I repented and rededicated my life back to Jesus Christ. Ever since that day, my daughter and I have become members and live on the ranch in the House of Leah. The Lord not only provided a place to stay for me and my daughter, but He also led me back to the place in which I had belonged a long time ago...back to a life of faith. Through the storm, the Lord delivered me and restored my soul."

Through prayer and love from her family members, especially her younger brother Rodrick, Curnara was able to return to her first love, Jesus Christ. He carried her through the storm to a safe place. And since then, she has become an essential part of our ministry. She now serves Him by singing as a leader on our Praise Team and she helps manage our Real New Orleans Style restaurants. Today, Curnara is seeking God deeper and more diligently then she's ever done before.

* * *

By bringing us to a new place to call home, God had proven once again that by trusting in Him, our feet were on solid ground. Jesus was the rock of our salvation, and the Holy Spirit was the comforter of our very souls. God, our provider, had blessed us as a ministry so that we could continue growing in His infinite wisdom, knowledge, and understanding. He had given us a land of peace, hope, and prosperity.

Not only had the Lord given us a facility for our worship services, Sunday school, fellowships, and prayer meetings, but He had also made provision for us to build brand new homes on the property for those who were interested in building. With that possibility open to us, I began negotiating with the Small Business Association for loan agreements to start the process of building roads for homes.

Man, getting the roads installed was a tough process. In July 2008, we finally started getting the roads put in. It was rough, but God worked it out. Our next steps were to get the waterlines installed, meet with potential builders for the houses, and seek lenders. This process proved to be time consuming as well, but it was just another test of our patience.

The Bible says in Hebrews 10:36, "For ye have need of patience, that, after ye have done the will of God, ye might receive the promise." God had already given us the land. We just needed to keep trusting, worshiping, and following in His footsteps. Personally, there were things that He'd promised and shown me that the ministry would possess someday. But of course, when God shows us things, sometimes it comes with a waiting season. Therefore, I just needed to continue to wait and believe that at the appointed time, the promises and vision would come to pass.

*   *   *

Through the rain and through the storms, God had a purpose for it all. He was restoring individual lives back to Himself and strengthening all of us along the way. Through the hurricanes and the wilderness experience, God was testing and proving our faith and allegiance to Him. I've noticed that whenever God had great plans for His people in the Bible, He usually brought them through the wilderness test, the dry place, before they could obtain the promises He had in store for them.

In our wilderness, the Lord was proving our hearts to see who was really for Him. At times, God was silent, and that was hard because it *seemed* like He wasn't there – but He was. He was simply watching and waiting to see if we were going to continue to follow His instruction and trust Him no matter what happened.

Even in times when we felt all alone, we knew that we could trust Him. We just had to believe, and that's not always an easy thing to do. We knew, though, that God was working things out on His end for our good. We just had to keep reminding ourselves of His past goodness and faithfulness. He was doing a lot during that time.

Not only was He bringing us through uncomfortable situations, He was also comforting us, healing past hurts, dealing with issues in our lives, and even strengthening relationships among brothers and sisters in Christ, mothers and daughters, husbands and wives, and even in-laws. Minister Julie Tumblin and her mother-in-law's relationship was strengthened through the miles, but it did not come free of hardship. She testifies:

Minister Julie

"Before the hurricanes, back in April 2002 and shortly after I'd married my husband, Elder William Tumblin, my mother-in-law, Alvera Tumblin was diagnosed with metastatic cancer. So immediately, I went from newlywed to caretaker. But I enjoyed taking care of her. When I took her to her weekly doctor appointments and chemotherapy, we would talk for hours and have good conversations. I believe that God allowed this illness to draw us closer together for various reasons unbeknown to either of us at that time. And when Hurricane Katrina was threatening to hit the city in 2005, we were faced with another test. She didn't want to leave. But we were not going to let her stay there when New Orleans was bracing for a dangerous Category Five hurricane. Over some time, we finally convinced her to leave. During the journey, I spent a lot of time with her while my husband helped retrieve things from Lumberton and New Orleans. During that time, I believed that the Lord spoke to me saying that He was going to heal my mother-in-law from cancer, which He later did. Praise the Lord! But in April 2008, her health started deteriorating again. She got sick, but this time there was a series of illnesses such as diabetes, MSRA, congestive heart failure, a heart attack, mini stroke, and several infections, and she later slipped into a coma, which she eventually came out of. She was a fighter, but I remember her telling me one day while we were alone that she was tired of fighting. She mentioned to me that whatever God's will was for her life, she desired it. So if that meant it was time for her to let go, then that is what she would do. Shortly afterwards, the doctors told us that there was nothing else that they could do for her. In April 2009, things spiraled downward, and Mother Tumblin passed away. It was a sad day for our family, but the Lord had prepared us long before. She'd accepted the Lord and lived for Him, went to church faithfully, and was one of the best dressed elderly women in the church. Through the storms and once we were settled, my mother-in-law and I really developed a loving relationship. We talked, laughed, and shared old stories all the time. She would share nuggets of wisdom from her life, like 'Ignorance is a hindering spirit.' I learned so much just by being in her company and watching her life. She really made an impact on my life and in the lives of so many others around her."

God is all about relationships, and Minister Julie's relationship with her mother-in-law is a great example of His love at work in people's lives. Mother Tumblin was a beautiful woman, and we all miss her very much, but we look forward to the awesome day when we will see her again in heaven.

It's amazing that in the midst of sorrow, the Lord has a way of bringing us joy. Psalm 30:5 says, "Weeping may endure for a night, but joy cometh in the morning." We know that it is nothing but the grace of God that gives us the strength to press on and endure the pain. Even though we may lose a lot in this life, we gain it back and more in Christ.

*   *   *

The Lord taught us a lot through the storm. He taught me true faith and how to really trust and rely on Him when the weather gets rough. I didn't always know what God was doing at certain points in the journey, and there were many times when I had to ask, "Lord, what am I to do with all of these people now? What next? I have never done this before. I need your help. I need your guidance. I need to hear your voice."And there was silence. But then when He was ready, He would grant me provision to lead us home.

Overall, I would have to conclude by saying that our exodus and experience through the storms was a journey in faith. It was a journey that we as a ministry could have never traveled alone. Jesus was with us. God never forsook us, left us, or failed us. He provided for us and carried us through every step of the way. We just needed to follow and trust in Him. That certainly wasn't easy after losing everything and becoming homeless in a matter of days, but the Lord kept us pressing strong through troubled and deep waters. He never let us go and He never let us fall. We never starved, grew thirsty, or truly lacked clothing. And when the fight to stand got rough, together we stood and continued to pray, sing praises unto the Lord, love, seek His face, and fight the good fight of faith. By this, He granted us His peace, protection, and constant provision. And in the end, we won! We made it! Through Jesus Christ, we made it!

And that is how, we as *one* church survived Hurricanes Katrina and Rita.

My lovely wife and I have been happily married and in the Lord together for over 20 years.

Pastor Willie Monnet, Sr. and Minister Claudette Monnet

Smoking for Jesus Ministry

"On Fire for the Lord"

Revelation 3:16

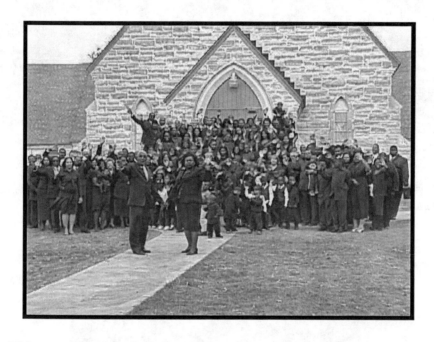

This was our church dedication and thanksgiving service unto the Lord for all that He'd done and brought us through…as well as the many blessings!

The Lord blessed us with 56 acres of land! This is our new church home in Burnet, Texas.

Lives are still being changed and
transformed on a weekly basis in Texas.
Our church doors are always open.

After five years of waiting, here are our homes finally
being built on the Land of Promise. We saw firsthand the
promises of God being fulfilled right before our very eyes.
He is faithful!

From the Pastor

Pastor Willie Monnet, Sr.

When Hurricane Katrina struck the city of New Orleans on Monday, August 29, 2005, it marked a turning point not only in our personal lives, but in our ministry as a whole. Looking back, I have come to the conclusion that from the beginning of time, God knew that this day would become a reality, and that it would shake the foundation of our nation and the very hearts of His people. It was a wake-up call!

Hurricane Katrina topped the records and claimed the title as *the* worst natural disaster in U.S. history. She came through like a hungry lion, claiming the lives of thousands, and left hundreds of thousands hungry, desperate, scattered, and homeless.

Over the years, many people have asked the questions, "Why would a loving God allow such a terrible thing to happen to New Orleans?" and "What was He doing through Katrina?" I believe the answer is that God had His hand on New Orleans. For so many years, God had been trying to draw men and women from the city to Himself and to a life surrendered to Jesus Christ. But many would not turn away from their sinful and wicked lifestyles. They wouldn't listen or even humble themselves to pray; instead, they only rejected Him more and more.

Some Christians had even become complacent in their walk with Christ – just going to church week after week, resisting the power to change. And our church was not exempt. God says in 2 Timothy 3:5 (NLT), "They will act religious, but they will reject the power that could make them godly. Stay away from people like that!" So God had to shake things up.

Many residents of New Orleans knew that the city was in dire need of a spiritual awakening. It had become such a dangerous place to live. The number of murders, armed robberies, and cases of corruption were growing, and on top of that, the city was full of immorality, upheld a failing educational system, and was possessed by a spirit of poverty. There was no fear of God there, and when I say no fear, I'm not talking about a "scary" type of fear but a reverential fear of God, a fear and respect for the awesome God who created all the earth and made all creation.

Who He is should be enough to stop all of us in our tracks to pause and consider the decisions we are about to make if they could cause us to sin against God and displease Him. We should always strive to do what pleases the Father. Sure, as Christians we make mistakes, but that's why we repent and ask the Holy Spirit to guide and lead us to not only hear the truth, but to obey it, lest we deceive ourselves (James 1:22). We have to make the choice to be willingly obedient and follow God's commands at all costs.

However, if we decide to quench the Spirit, or continue to reject Him and His power to change us, then we are left in God's hands. 1 Samuel 12:15 says, "But if ye will not obey the voice of the Lord, but rebel against the commandment of the Lord, then shall the hand of the Lord be against you, as it was against your fathers." So make no mistake about it, God is loving, but He is also just.

* * *

Through the storms and all the devastation, God still poured out His unconditional love, unmerited favor, and delivering power upon many. Yes, we may have lost most of our natural possessions, but we still had our lives, each other, and most importantly, our salvation.

I kept reminding myself that God had a greater plan in store for us, and running from two hurricanes while traveling the state of Texas was a part of it. We had to make the exodus from New Orleans to get through the wilderness to inherit the promises of God.

In this life, there are wilderness experiences. Although the way of the wilderness is far from easy, the refining process of purification, transformation, and restoration changes our lives for the better. In the season of preparation, God molds and shapes us to receive His promises, and then He brings us to the wilderness to test His mold and make sure it's strong enough to receive those promises. That's why it was so important for us not to grumble about what God was doing in our lives.

He knew the plans that He had for us, plans to prosper us, not to harm us, but to give us a hope and a future (Jeremiah 29:11 NIV). We just had to wait on Him patiently, cling tightly to our faith, and trust that the God who had delivered the Israelites in Moses' day was the same God who could deliver us today. He said in Malachi 3:6 (NLT), "I am the Lord, and I do not change," and in 1 Peter 5:7 (NLT), His Word reads, "Give all your worries and cares to God, for He cares about you."

God provided for us in every way imaginable. He delivered us and blended us together into a new community, and He continued to bless us in a new land. His Word is true when it says, "I have never seen the righteous forsaken or their children begging bread" (Psalm 37:25 NIV). The Lord had provided shelter for our bodies, food for our bellies, clothes for our backs, shoes for our feet, and He blessed us with His unmerited favor and faithfulness!

* * *

God definitely revealed His supernatural power through the storm – power to cleanse, power to heal, and power to rebuild and redirect. We were caught off guard by the method He used to show us His power, but without a doubt we have grown closer to Him through these experiences.

Looking back, perhaps we shouldn't have been quite so surprised by the events that occurred. Early in 2005, I had prophesied that New Orleans would be hit by a bad hurricane, and that most certainly happened. Our church members had been building their faith through the teachings and studies within our church, and they had been putting that faith to practice outside of the church walls. God had been preparing us all that time; we just hadn't realized it yet.

We were not only warned of it in the spiritual sense, but we were also warned in the natural by meteorologists and weather trackers for years. Nevertheless, we went on with our daily lives as though nothing would ever happen.

I believe that this is how it will be when Jesus Christ returns. People will have been warned in the spiritual and in the natural, but as they go about their daily lives, He will come unexpectedly like a thief in the night to take His church (1 Thessalonians 5:2-4). This day is known by many theologians and Bible scholars as the Rapture of the Church. And for this, we want to be ready…at all times! The Bible says in 1 Thessalonians 4:16-17 (NLT):

> "For the Lord Himself will come down from heaven with
> a commanding shout, with the voice of the archangel, and
> with the trumpet call of God. First, the Christians who
> have died will rise from their graves. Then, together with
> them, we who are still alive and remain on the earth will be
> caught up in the clouds to meet the Lord in the air. Then
> we will be with the Lord forever."

That will be one of the *greatest* evacuations this world has ever seen! But this time we won't need three days' worth of clothing, medical records, pillows, blankets, snacks for the road, or hotel accommodations, because we'll be gone in the twinkling of an eye (1 Corinthians 15:52). The world will be devastated and in chaos! The tribulation hour will have begun and many will have been left behind who didn't believe in, accept, or live for Jesus Christ. Matthew 24:40-41 (NLT) says, "Two men will be working together in the field; one will be taken, the other left. Two women will be grinding flour at the mill; one will be taken, the other left." Now is the time to repent of our sins because the Kingdom of Heaven is near (Matthew 3:2).

* * *

As mentioned in the introduction, all of the signs are upon us. The Bible says in Matthew 24:7, "For nation shall rise against nation, and kingdom against kingdom: and there shall be famines, and pestilences, and earthquakes, in divers places." Currently, our spiritual eyes are being opened more and more as we see the Scriptures coming to pass through an increase in tragedies, including 9/11, Indonesia's tsunami, Hurricane Katrina, heightened terrorist alerts, talks of peace while war is more rampant than ever, famines, diseases, the 2008 economic crisis, and the unexpected earthquakes that shook Haiti, Chile, and China – all signs pointing to the fact that Jesus is coming soon and, in preparation, shouting a warning to people everywhere to draw near to Him.

The only question that should be asked now is if we will take heed to these warnings and be ready, because I truly believe that His Coming is very near and fast approaching. The Scriptures remind us of this fact: "Take ye heed, watch and pray: for ye know not when the time is" (Mark 13:33).

*   *   *

Today, I believe God is preparing the body of Christ for one of the greatest revivals this world has ever seen. And not like the tent revival that we drove nine hours to attempt to do in New Orleans for the third year anniversary of Hurricane Katrina. That was a wild experience within itself, because Hurricane Gustav was right upon our heels. But that didn't stop our efforts. The Praise Team kept singing and I kept on preaching, even as we witnessed the highway filling up beside us. As time went on, we realized that our trip was not in vain at all, because several souls were saved that weekend. Hallelujah! After that, it was time to hit the road for another long exodus. Only this time, we knew exactly where we were headed…back *home* to Burnet, Texas. God was faithful once more.

We sing a song in our church services sometimes called "Get Ready for Revival" by Jonathan Stockstill. In the song, there's a part where we sing, "Can you feel it? Can you feel the fire? Do you want it? Do you want the fire?" And then people of God sing, "Yes, I want it! Yes, I want it! Yes, I want the fire!"

That's what God wants all of us to say: "Yes, Lord, purify my soul, change me from the inside out, make me a person who fears You and pleases You, Oh Lord. Show me Your ways and make me whole." He wants to know that we know that we need Him to survive, and that we can do nothing without Him.

Through these storms, these natural disasters, and our traveling, God was purifying our hearts and setting us apart to make us true disciples to the life of faith in Jesus Christ. And even now after the storms, He's still working on us. As followers of Christ, through His strength and grace, our lives will be full of God's incredible transformations, of His deliverance and amazing freedom! The Bible says, "For the Lord is the Spirit, and wherever the Spirit of the Lord is, there is freedom. So all of us who have had that veil removed can see and reflect the glory of the Lord. And the Lord—who is the Spirit—makes us more and more like Him as we are changed into His glorious image" (2 Corinthians 3:17-18 NLT).

I hear a lot of talk today about rebuilding New Orleans, the American economy, Haiti, Chile, and China, but we must never forget the Master Rebuilder. Jesus wants to rebuild us and restore us back to His Father. That was the plan from the beginning of time, even before Adam and Eve messed up in the garden.

He is the Master Carpenter. Back in His days on earth, He was always rebuilding and fixing up things. Well, that hasn't changed. He is still in the rebuilding business. He rebuilds hearts, broken relationships, bank accounts, severed marriages, homes, businesses, churches, and the list goes on and on. This is all done, simply because He loves us.

We know this firsthand, because after five years, the Lord has blessed us tremendously by rebuilding our lives and church in Burnet County, and allowed us to reestablish the Smokehouse Restaurant with its *new* name, The Real New Orleans Style Restaurant where we have three locations in Marble Falls, Round Mountain, and Burnet, Texas (all within a 30 mile radius from each other). In addition, the Lord has also begun reconstructing our lives by blessing us with the building of our new homes near the church. We are truly seeing the promises being fulfilled right before our very eyes! It's all coming to pass! So I know that if the Lord could do this for us, then He can certainly do it for many, many others. Jesus is the same yesterday, today and forever (Hebrews 13:8).

Our story is one that tells of God's delivering and keeping power! Even though *we'd* lost everything, *He* restored us and rebuilt our lives back up again in a new place. God allowed storms like Hurricanes Katrina and Rita along with other hardships to draw us and others to Himself and to His

Son, Jesus Christ. He wants us to change our mindsets and our hearts and rely solely on Him to be our source of strength, peace, and protection in the midst of trouble, no matter what shape or form it may come in.

We have certainly learned that lesson at Smoking for Jesus Ministry. As a result, we are even more on fire for the Lord (Rev. 3:15-16)! God has refreshed us and purified our souls, and He's making us whole again every day. Through the storm, the Lord carried us safely through our own wilderness experience all across Texas, and we crossed our own modern-day Jordan into the Hill Country. This is the true story of how *one* church survived Hurricanes Katrina and Rita…a story that we will never forget, and will be told from generation to generation.

"Meet the Members"

Minister Doris Mosley

Minister Doris Mosley:
Rebuilding a Shattered Life

Before Hurricane Katrina, I had been a member of Smoking for Jesus Ministry for ten years. I came into the church doors at 22 years of age as a single mother of one. I was depressed, empty, and broken. I felt as though my life had been shattered into a thousand pieces. I was overcome with suicidal thoughts due to deep rooted hurts of abuse, rejection and fear, which stemmed from my troubled early childhood and teenage years. I needed help. I needed healing. I longed to be put back together again…to be made whole. But I didn't know how to rebuild my life, until, one day, my next door neighbor handed me the audio teaching series on *The Word of God* from Pastor Willie Monnet, Sr. of Smoking for Jesus Ministry.

That series marked a turning point in my life. I was so enlightened by the Word of the Lord that I visited a Wednesday night service, rededicated my life, and ever since that day, my life has never been the same. They welcomed me with open and loving arms, and offered me and my daughter a place to live in the House of Leah (a ministry within our ministry, which is purposefully designed to provide a spiritual covering for single women who need shelter, guidance, and restoration). I have to admit that when I first walked through those doors, I carried a lot of baggage. I was bitter, unforgiving, unloving, and I was afraid to let anyone see inside of my life. I was a woman who was emotionally broken, physically tired, and spiritually lifeless. My heart had so many fortified walls that needed to be torn down. I needed to be reconstructed.

During my stay, we had weekly Bible studies and counseling sessions, and I attended single's ministry monthly. There, I was also able to build an intimate relationship with my Lord and Savior, Jesus Christ. As the years went on, the baggage began to fall off, the walls were coming down, and I began to lay down every weight that slowed me down and every sin that hindered my progress to running the race that God had set before me (Hebrews 12:1). So when Hurricane Katrina blew through, I was already trained to weather the storm *spiritually*. During the journey, I actually was able to draw even closer to God, which refreshed my spirit and increased my faith in the Lord.

Today, after the storm, I am a free woman. I'm free from the bondage of depression, fear, and rejection. Since then, the Lord has blessed me with a godly husband, I have a blended family now in which we are raising our two children up in the admonition of the Lord, and I am also an intercessor and minister of the gospel of Jesus Christ. My life has been rebuilt! All glory belongs to God!

Erin Legier

Erin Legier:
A Story of Restoration

On Thursday, August 25, 2005, while my family and I were wrapping up our vacation in Florida, we got word that the same small hurricane that had already hit in south Florida was now headed back into the Gulf of Mexico, and weather forecasters were now predicting that she'd strike New Orleans. Initially, we laughed it off, because people were in such an uproar about it; in the past, we'd run from several storms, yet nothing bad ever happened. So we figured this was just another scare. But when we got home and looked at the news late Friday evening, we noticed that Katrina was gaining strength and was calculated to become a dangerous Category Five hurricane by Sunday, and was scheduled to strike on Monday.

Shortly thereafter, I got a call from the ministry's planning coordinator telling us that our church was planning to leave together early Sunday morning. Now, I had been a member of Smoking for Jesus Ministry for four years prior to Hurricane Katrina's threat. I remember walking into the church doors when my life was in shambles. I had been working in the restaurant industry for about 10 years, but I was having trouble with my job, I had money problems, and I was separated from my wife due to some tough marital issues. My life, I felt, was in ruins and had become very unfulfilling.

But God used this ministry and my pastor to restore my soul by teaching me the uncompromising Word of God week after week, laboring with me through prayer, giving me a job in the church-owned Smokehouse Restaurant (where I later became manager), and gave me a shelter to not only lay my head at night, but a spiritual covering to strengthen my soul and spirit in the House of Joseph, a place for single men to get their lives on track naturally and spiritually. As a result, I was able to get back on my feet financially, I learned how to be a true godly man, a responsible father, and God restored my marriage after being separated for ten years.

So when Hurricane Katrina was coming, there our pastor was again – ready to extend an open invitation to travel with him, his family, and the church body to a safe place. He was selfless. And I am so thankful that we did decide to travel with our church, because together, we were all able to see firsthand the move of God on our behalf. Even after losing everything through the storm, I've gained so much more. Today, God has strengthened my marriage and family, reestablished the restaurant in Texas with its new name, the Real New Orleans Style Restaurant which I manage, and I am currently training to become a minister of the gospel of Jesus Christ. Through God, all things are possible!

04/04/2010

Derriel Collins

DERRIEL COLLINS:
FREEDOM RAIN

I was only eleven years old when my family and I evacuated for Hurricane Katrina to Lumberton. I didn't know what to expect from the storm, because I was pretty young at the time. My family was new to the ministry, so I didn't have any friends. I wasn't very familiar with anyone in the youth group yet, so it was scary for me. It was a different place. But once we got settled in, one of the girls in the youth group named Jeanecia introduced herself to me and almost instantly we became friends. It made it a lot easier to have someone to talk to every night.

Over time, as we traveled from place to place, I was able to loosen up with the other kids, and I did a lot better than I thought. We actually had fun! We laughed, joked around, watched television, and played games to help pass the time. They helped me to get out of my shell and open up more. I realized that it was fun being a Christian. Sure, I had my share of problems. I didn't have a close relationship with my stepdad and I missed my family in New Orleans, especially my grandmother. Through the years, though, things have changed dramatically in my life.

Today, after the rain and devastation of Hurricanes Katrina and Rita, I am living a life of freedom in Jesus Christ. I am 16 years old, the oldest of four siblings, and here in Marble Falls, I have adapted to my church, youth group, and high school very well. I am also in the dance ministry, which I love, because I can express my worship to the Lord freely this way. Also, after much prayer, my family members, including my grandmother, have moved up here and have even accepted Jesus Christ as their Lord and Savior.

It gets even better. In addition to that, in 2008, me and my special friend entered into a courtship program called *Young Love Courtship* at our church. I like this program because, unlike dating, we're courting. With dating, you go for what you know, but with courting, there are spiritual limits and boundaries. It keeps us safe and grounded in the things of God. Through praying together, journaling, communicating over the phone, counseling, single's ministry, youth group, and supervised outings, we're able to get to know one another better, all the while being free from the hurting relationships, premarital sex, diseases, and pregnancies outside of wedlock. This is not a try-it-before-you-buy-it program. It's a *true love waits* program. We want to remain pure until marriage. And we're enjoying it. The storm really changed my life and made me a better person. I can honestly say that now, I am free in Christ.

David and Wendy Armour

David and Wendy Armour:
In the Master's Hands

Our story is about obedience and endurance. No matter how hard it got during the storm, we never gave up on the Lord, and He never gave up on us. The whole time, our family was rooted and grounded in the ministry that God had planted us in since the year 2000, and through our faithfulness to the Lord and to a pastor after God's own heart, we were carried safely in the Master's hands.

David

Six days before we evacuated for Hurricane Katrina, my wife had a C-section and gave birth to twin baby girls. When it came time to leave the city, we didn't have any money, and we didn't have a car. Yet, the Lord provided for our every need. He never let us down. As we remained obedient to His Word, and trusted in the fact that He was going to take care of us, we didn't have need to worry. I knew that God was doing something awesome through this storm. I believe that He was rerouting us to align us with His plans and purposes for our lives. But He had to get us out of our comfort zones. During that time, we needed to be sensitive to God's will for our lives. I knew that the Lord had great things in store for us through this ministry.

Wendy

Five years after the storm, God still hasn't failed us. We're living in Marble Falls, Texas, and still pressing through and trying to stay in the center of God's will. My husband is working in the ministry full time now as a cook at the Real New Orleans Style Restaurant, a grade school teacher at Smoking for Jesus Ministry Christian School, writing a book, and in training to become a minister of the gospel. And the Lord has blessed me with a business called Ribbons of Glory. Today, we are blessed! Our children are healthy and we're doing what God has called us to do in the right place and at the right time.

Viola Chapman

Viola Chapman:
The Eye of the Storm

Three months before Hurricane Katrina hit, I had a dream that the Superdome cracked open and there was this great flood. The city of New Orleans was under twenty feet of water, and a lot of people drowned. The dream started out with God telling me to go up, and I would go to the second floor of the building I was in, and then He'd say, "No, go up higher." Until I ended up on the roof, and then He said, "Watch," and the Superdome cracked open and the water came pouring out of it. There were children walking home from school and parents were out there too, and I was yelling, "The water is coming! Danger! Danger!" But nobody listened. They just kept walking by. Then suddenly, the water came rushing in, and they were all washed away. Yet when the water receded, the people were still there on the ground. But they were lifeless. And then the Lord said, "I come in the twinkling of an eye." The dream startled me so that I even shared it with a few of my co-workers at the Smokehouse Restaurant several days later. It was as if God was allowing me to see what was about to happen.

And on Sunday, August 28, 2005, I found myself evacuating with the church, running from the coming storm. I remember it like it was yesterday. As we were driving away to Lumberton, I just kept thinking about what was going to happen to my family, home, church, and our city. I guess because the dream was in my subconscious mind, I sensed very strongly that I wasn't going back. I just had this overwhelming feeling that things weren't going to be the same anymore. However, I quickly snapped back into reality and laid aside everything that I was feeling inside. I needed to place my trust and hope in Jesus Christ. I needed to cling to my faith and believe that God was our provider, and no matter what happened, He was going to take care of us. And He did just that!

Looking back through the journal that I kept throughout the journey, I remember writing in so many words that when this was all said and done, that the Lord was going to bring us into a land of promise. Believe it or not, after five years, the Lord has blessed us as a church with our new subdivision called the Land of Promise! What an awesome God we serve!

In the end, the dream was a sign that God was *not only* going to see me safely through the storm to higher ground, but that He was going to bring me to another level of faith in my walk with Him. Today, I am thankful to be alive to *see* the Lord's continual blessings shine forth not only in my life, but also in the lives of so many others around me.

Additional Members of Smoking for Jesus Ministry

Above is Usher Simeon Williams, Desmond Green accepting the Lord Jesus Christ with Pastor Monnet. Below is Desmond with his sister Curnara Green at Hurricane Katrina's 3rd year anniversary tent revival in New Orleans.

From (l) to (r) are Minister Charmaine Richard, LPN Nurse Viola
Chapman, RN Nurse Anitra Torns, Elder William Tumblin, and
Minister Julie Tumblin. Also below are Azariah, Moriah, and
Gabrielle Sordelet, and Darian and Feandrell Brown.

1st row: Juanita Fraise, Eronie White, Alvera Tumblin, and Calvin and Courtnaye Richard; 2nd row: Sean, Donita, Sean, Jr., Shante', and Shanice Richard and Christine, Erin, Isaac, and Brandon Legier; 3rd row: Josiah, Dedrick, and Trenae Thompson and Tiffany Thomas.

Above: Sylvia Cressy and Erika Chapman; Lavonda and Zion Eaglin. Middle are Minister Janice Williams, Brenda Woods, Minister Tara Griffin, and Viola Chapman. Below from (l) to (r): Brenda Woods, Trenae Thompson, Sylvia Cressy, Carol Smothers, and Racheal Frazier; and Karen Baptiste and Bobbette Boyd.

Above is our SFJM Christian rap group "Sound Minds"- 1ˢᵗ
row: Johnnel Mosley, Minister Marvin and wife Demaries
Glaspie, Charles Frazier, Derrick Washington, Simeon
Williams, Paige Roberson, and Tiffany Thomas; 2ⁿᵈ row:
David Armour, Darian Brown, Minister Johnny Mosley,
and Johnny Williams. Bottom picture are SFJM ushers: (l)
to (r) Sean Richard, Anthony Torns, Viola Chapman,
Deacon Eddie Roberson, Travonda Woods, David Armour,
Simeon Williams, and Deacon Ralph Woods.

172

SFJM Ministers - 1st row: Erick and Stacy Brown, Marvin Glaspie, Charmaine and Calvin J. Richard, Sr., Elder William Tumblin and Julie Tumblin, Johnny Mosley, Tara and Gaylin Griffin, and Janice and Dwight Williams; 2nd row: Doris Mosley, Minister Claudette Monnet, Pastor Willie Monnet Sr., and Everett Sanders. Below: SFJM Children's Ministry.

SFJM Youth Ministry: Youth Ablaze on the playground
at the church.

THE SMOKING FOR JESUS MINISTRY JOURNEY

Pastor Willie Monnet, Sr.
& Minister Claudette Monnet
Elder William Tumblin
Minister Julie Tumblin
Alvera Tumblin
Briana Fisher
Brian Fisher
Juliette Fisher
David Armour
Wendy Armour
Makala Armour
Malachi Armour
Honor Armour
Majesty Armour
Eddie Roberson
Andrea Roberson
Paige Roberson
Jireh Roberson
Eronie White
Herschel White
Juanita Fraise
Joan Delaney
Wilbert Delaney
Erick Brown
Stacy Brown
Dwayne Smothers
Carol Smothers
Barbara Davis
Conrad Lawrence

Corey Smith
Yniska Smith
William Ford
Ella Ford
Bobbette Boyd
Trinity Boyd
Laquinta Grady
Brian Grady
Bryonika Grady
Derrick Davis
Jovan Davis
Jalashawn Davis
Derrion Davis
Charles Green
Kizzy Green
Charles Green, Jr.
Derriel Collins
Damon Collins Green
Tiffany Thomas
Shakirra Hall
Johnny Mosley
Terra Mosley
Johnny Mosley, Jr.
Jahday Mosley
Joshua Mosley
Viola Chapman
Erika Chapman
Brandi Noah
Myrianna Taylor

Dominic Noah
Dwight Williams
Janice Williams
Briara Williams
Dwight Williams, Jr.
Charles Fraizer
Racheal Frazier
Alysia Frazier
Rebecca Frazier
Nya'Mia Frazier
Charles Frazier
Jonathan Frazier
Arthur Eaglin
Lavonda Eaglin
Zynarrea Johnson
Arthur Eaglin, Jr.
Erin Legier
Christine Legier
Brandon Legier
Isaac Legier
Devin Legier
Anthony Torns
Anitra Torns
Anthony Torns, Jr.
Alexis Torns
Ashton Torns
Dedrick Thompson
Trenae Thompson
Josiah Thompson
Feandrell Sordelet
Gabrielle Sordelet
Azariah Sordelet
Moriah Sordelet
Keith Jerome
Akira Jerome

Sharde Jerome
Keith Jerome, Jr.
Johnnel Mosley
Lauren Mosley
Israel Mosley
Marvin Glaspie, Jr.
Demaries Glaspie
Marvin Glaspie, III
Joshua Brown
Caleb Brown
Royale Brown
Sean Richard
Donita Richard
Shante Richard
Shanice Richard
Sean Richard, Jr.
Ralph Woods
Brenda Woods
Therron Jerome
Ralph Woods, Jr.
Jill Hewitt
Everett Sanders
Darlene Sanders
Eric Sanders
Quinton Sanders
Minister Doris Edwards
Jeanecia Edwards
Edith Boyd
Brion Boyd
Nia Boyd
Eliza Johnson
Thelma Cowart
Derrick Washington
Ernest Schuster
Darian Brown

Johnny Williams
Rodrick Green
Simeon Williams
Obadiah Williams
Luke Roy
Gavin Roth
Minister June Roth
Cyril Lemon
Joseph Brown, Jr.
Patrice Brown
Jonathan Brown
Jamal Brown
Brandon Brown
Ronald Sims
Catherine Smith
Darron Woods
Travonda Woods
Joseph Woods

Savior Woods
Naomi Woods
Jillian Lawrence
Christopher Jenkins
Sharron Summeral
Sharde Summeral
Shelina Smith
Minister Calvin J. Richard, Sr.
Minister Charmaine Richard
Calvin J. Richard, Jr.
Courtnaye Richard
Cali Richard
Armond Pierre
Minister Gayln Griffin, Sr.
Minister Tara Griffin
Jaye'lyn Griffin
Gayln Griffin, Jr.
Bryant Ross

And a host of extended family members and friends

www.mountupbook.com

Smoking For Jesus Ministry Rev. 3:16
"On Fire for the LORD"
Elder Willie Monnet, Sr. - Pastor
1804 FM 2342 - Burnet, Texas 78611
(512) 756-1712 or (504) 242-3680   Toll Free (866) 756-1712
Web Site: WWW.SMOKINGFORJESUSMINISTRY.ORG

Sunday School 8:00 am	**Worship Service 9:15 am**
For All Ages	*Nursery Provided (6 mos. - 5 yrs.)*

Saturday Corporate Prayer 4:45 pm
Men's Bible Study - Monday - 7:00 pm (Males Only)
Discipleship Class - Wednesday - 7:00 pm (All Are Welcome)

LaVergne, TN USA
03 August 2010
191851LV00002B/2/P

9 781452 024158